Best wishes

Keith Newman.

'Hacking It'

TALES OF A VERY PROVINCIAL NEWSPAPER JOURNALIST

Keith Newbery

Portman Publishing and Communications Limited
Suffolk Studios, 284 Ravenswood Avenue,
Ipswich IP3 9TQ

First published in Great Britain in 2003 by
Portman Publishing and Communications Limited

A catalogue record for this book is
available from the British Library

ISBN 0 9545881 0 X

Typeset in Sabon, and printed in Great Britain by
Printwise (Haverhill) Limited, Suffolk

First Edition (November 2003)

www.portman.uk.com/books

This is for my parents, Jack and Doris, with love and thanks for providing me with the chance they never had.

Contents

Chichester Observer

Foreword

DO YOU TAKE your local paper? I do and I am fortunate in having a very good paper with a very good editor.

Not all others are of comparable standard, some are carelessly produced, some are insipid, some have an amateurish look. Ultimately everything depends upon the editor, and ever since he took over in Chichester, years ago now, Keith Newbery has maintained an exceptionally high standard. He is never afraid to speak his mind, and to read some of his comments is like breathing in fresh air.

There have been many humorous episodes, in one of which I was involved. I had been having fun with the Southern Gas company, who threatened to sue me for non-payment of a bill to repair the central heating in my house - blissfully regardless of the fact that my home is gasless and relies entirely on oil to keep it warm.

The Gas Man came to see me. I had invited Keith to be present - and as soon as my visitor realised there was a journalist in the room he was through the front door like greased lightning. The entire interview lasted for exactly 19 seconds!

But there have been many serious interviews too, and Keith is unfailingly courteous and fair-minded. He is well aware that a local paper has immense power to do good and to campaign for common sense - as was shown recently when he led the campaign against a decision by Chichester council to cut back on dustbin collection, thereby allowing evil-smelling rubbish to pile up for protracted periods.

He has been critical of the Sussex Police, who are very interested in bullying motorists but much less successful in catching burglars and vandals. He publishes an extremely good colour supplement each week and he makes sure all his facts are correct. (Not once have I been described as an astrologer!)

Being a journalist is far from easy. You have to be honest, firm, skilful and hard-working. Keith has all these qualities and the people who live in our area owe him great deal.

I wish him well with this book.

Sir Patrick Moore
Selsey, West Sussex
September 2003

Acknowledgments

THERE IS AN old cliché that would have us believe everyone has a book inside them. Well I haven't any longer, because this is it. It's been a long time coming for one very good reason - writing is extremely hard work, I have never particularly enjoyed doing it and envy those who actually get some pleasure from what I have always found to be an arduous business.

I only ever do it because I have to, and on this occasion I eventually got worn down by family and friends who insisted I write this book. When I asked why, they replied: "Because then you won't have to tell us all these bloody stories any more."

That was as good a reason as any, so I would like to thank my wife Denise, my son Mark and my daughter Sam for nagging me into it, and my old mate Mike Bull for ringing up at regular intervals and saying: "You haven't forgotten this have you?" And I always had.

My thanks also to Sir Patrick Moore for finding the time in his hectic life to provide the foreword and to my employers Johnston Press for their help in the sale and promotion of this book. No expression of gratitude can be too great for Dave Bowers, who undertook the proof-reading chore despite having heard most of this stuff a dozen times before.

Finally, my thanks to publisher Michael Lenihan, an unlikely angel but he went where others feared to tread and put his money where my mouth is. I hope it works out for both of us.

Keith Newbery
Winford, Isle of Wight
September 2003

PREFACE

And some are more equal than others...

AGRICULTURAL SHOWS HAVE a smell all their own. Country people find something timeless and reassuring about the waft of animal waste, leather, fried onions, damp canvas and traction engine fumes. Better still if it is accompanied by the mournful baying of various animals, a PA system burbling indistinctly in the background and a low babble of conversation that gets increasingly raucous as trade in the beer tent builds to an early-evening crescendo.

As a junior reporter on the Isle of Wight in the sixties, I recall the Island show being marked in the office diary as imperishably as Christmas. Each year, on the appointed day, up to half a dozen reporters and photographers representing the local weekly, the *County Press*, and the two evenings based in Portsmouth and Southampton, would converge on the site halfway between Newport and Cowes. Once there, we would gather in our own little tent and immediately begin to sort out life's priorities.

The lads from the evenings would go off in search of a story for that day's paper, and return with the same one they had written for each of the past ten years. 'Bright sunshine/overcast conditions greeted early arrivals to the Isle of Wight Agricultural show, which has this year attracted a record/disappointing number of entries.' (Delete where applicable). Meanwhile, the less driven representatives of the *County Press*, who had all that day and most of the following week to cobble together their compelling prose about the gymkhana, the rabbit show and the contest between apparently sane men to discover who could saw through a log fastest, dealt with their own needs.

'Are they providing lunch this year or do we have to forage for ourselves?' 'Anyone got any matches?' 'Is that coffee I can smell?' 'Have you finished with that *Mirror*?' 'Why do they always put this bloody tent on the opposite side of the ground from the toilets?' The chuntering would continue as typewriters were unpacked and ballpoints borrowed. Then we would venture forth with notebooks at the ready to meet familiar friends and write old stories about new animals.

This particular year, there was a stranger in our midst. He had been shipped over to cover the event from one of the *Portsmouth Evening News'* mainland offices. He was a slightly stout, bearded young man with fashionably large glasses that he had to keep pushing back up to the bridge of his nose, rather like Eric Morecambe. This meant his head was permanently tilted back at a rather superior angle. He also had that air of assertive bumptiousness that is common to most journalists, especially those attempting to establish themselves in the company of strangers. And in the mid-sixties the company did not come much stranger than a group of Island-based reporters trying desperately to extract a news story from an event that had not provided one for at least 40 years.

The newcomer slid his glasses back up his nose, cocked his head to one side and gazed morosely around the field. 'So this is what passes for a social life on the Isle of Wight,' he said.

It is impossible to be born on the Island without developing an ability to laugh at yourself. Rather like the Irish in the rest of Britain and the Poles in America, Islanders take naturally to the role of comedy stooge. Tell people you come from the Isle of Wight, and within seconds they will either mention in-breeding or inquire whether we yet have access to electricity. As a defence mechanism, Islanders have now taken to getting in first by making up jokes about themselves.

'Do you mean you've never attended a concert given by the Isle of Wight Symphony Orchestra?' I demand of strangers. 'You haven't lived until you've heard 60 boss-eyed people all playing the banjo at the same time.'

'In-breeding on the Isle of Wight?' I snort indignantly. 'There's no such thing. If you don't believe me just ask my mother, cousin Nigel.'

One look at the stranger in our midst convinced me of the need to take up just such a defensive position, and jokes at my own expense began to gather in the back of my mind ready for deployment. 'Not exactly the best place to break in a pair of new suede shoes,' he said, gazing down ruefully at his feet, which were ensnared by grubby clumps of long, damp grass.

'You didn't volunteer for this lot then?'

'Christ no. Got the short straw. The countryside's for looking at, not being in, as far as I'm concerned. Give me the mean streets of Gosport any time. Chris Cramer by the way.'

He extended his hand, and that was how I first met the man who 20 years later was to become one of the most high-profile journalists in the world.

Cramer went on to become the managing editor of the American network CNN and I went on to become the editor of a number of different weekly newspapers in the south of England. You could say we both found our natural level, but it goes to prove that as far as journalism is concerned, everyone starts equal before, as Orwell so shrewdly observed, some go on to be more equal than others.

I recall seeing Cramer trudge away from the Island showground that evening. He was a man who never seemed to be in a hurry, except where his career was concerned. He next came to my attention about 12 years later when he was working for the BBC. With perfect timing, he happened to be visiting the Iranian embassy in London on that May day in 1980 when it was taken over by terrorists. Twenty-six people had been taken hostage including the bemused Cramer who had only popped in to collect a visa and suddenly found himself cast as a reluctant pawn in a dramatic incident that was watched live on television screens around the world and was always destined to end in bloodshed.

Cramer (and who can blame him?) quickly concluded that a prudent outbreak of self-preservation was called for, and 24 hours later was filmed being hauled through the streets of London on a stretcher, apparently in the throes of a severe stomach virus alleged to have been contracted in Africa some months earlier. I was watching the coverage with my father, who had survived Dunkirk and had little sympathy for journalists as a breed, and none whatsoever for those that were pretending to be ill. 'I'm not surprised he's got guts trouble,' said the old chap. 'Most people would get the shits if they were faced with half a dozen Arabs carrying rifles and hand grenades.'

He was closer to the truth than he could have known. Years later Cramer admitted that though he had been feeling 'a little under the weather' he had 'ramped it up a bit' to win his release.

The last time I saw him was when he was beamed in from the States to take part in the *This is Your Life* programme featuring John Humphrys. He looked like your typical all-American, middle-aged professional guy who showed every sign of having embraced a clutch of youth-giving therapies. He was tanned and trim, and flaunted a discernible chin and a chippy expression. Apparently he and Humphrys had been good mates during their early days at the BBC, and the respect and gratitude with which Humphrys received his contribution confirmed that I had indeed been in the presence of nascent greatness in that soggy Isle of Wight field more than 30 years before.

Incidentally, there is an amusing tailpiece to the story of the Iranian siege. During the six days in which the drama unfolded, a local radio sports reporter phoned his news desk to ask how things were going at the Embassy. He was referring to the world snooker championships and was somewhat startled to be informed: 'The SAS have gone in and they reckon there are several dead.'

Cramer's life has been one of jetting around the world, deploying hundreds of staff to various flash-points and making a personal friend of people like Jane Fonda. Mine has been one of travelling backwards and forwards across the Solent, getting people to submit flower-show reports on time and for nothing, and making a personal enemy of Peter Mandelson.

You could say that one of us got what he wanted, the other got what he deserved. But the thing about journalism is that it matters not whether you bestride the world stage or crouch in your little corner of the provinces, it is a job that is gloriously unpredictable. Like Cramer I suspect, I have met some life-enhancing characters, some charlatans, some heroes and some poseurs. And that's just the people I've worked with.

I've interviewed people whose company I would not wish upon my worst enemies and chatted at length with others like Mo Mowlam, Patrick Moore and Michael Parkinson who have made the job worthwhile. More important still, I have encountered local characters who didn't know they were and some genuine eccentrics who have burned themselves into my memory with their antics and attitude.

I also have the honour of being the reporter who, despatched by his news desk to write the first piece on the tanker Pacific Glory that was ablaze off the Isle of Wight, stood everyone down by telling them the fire on board had gone out. Weeks later it was still smouldering away, and to this day I cannot recall that moment without feeling the blood gush up through my neck and into my ears.

This is not an autobiography; you have to have achieved something important to consider yourself worthy of compiling such a thing. No, this is just a collection of memories and anecdotes; some personal and some passed on to me for safe-keeping. I have no idea whether those in the latter category are true. I only know that I was told they were. But then again, it was journalists who told me.

Whether they are true or not is not really the issue. I found them amusing and I hope I have been able to convey a little of that to you.

This is not a book for which any research was required. As I started to write it, people and events that were worthy of recall came to mind.

If I didn't remember somebody or something, it was presumably because it or they were not funny, touching or dramatic enough to have made a lasting impression. That is not to say that I have forgotten all the other people I have worked with over the past 37 years, far from it. They have comprised the agreeable backcloth, content to leave the centre stage to the more flamboyant characters whose company we have all enjoyed.

CHAPTER ONE

Now which bank would you like to work for?

THE INVITATION WAS embossed, expensive and featured my name spelled incorrectly. I was immediately touched by how far the organisers of the British Press Awards were prepared to go to make a hack from the sticks feel at home.

The year was 1981 and I had been summoned to the annual lunch at the Savoy where I had been shortlisted in the Critic of the Year category. This jamboree was usually the exclusive preserve of the Fleet Street glitterati, and my fellow nominees certainly fell into this category. They were Clive James (then of the *Observer*), Nancy Banks-Smith (*Guardian*) and Herbert Kretzmer (*Daily Mail*).

All went well until the nominations were announced. 'Clive James of the *Observer*.' (Applause and cheers). 'Nancy Banks-Smith of the *Guardian*.' (Applause and even louder cheers). 'Herbert Kretzmer of the *Daily Mail*' (Applause and polite murmurs). 'Keith Newbery, *The News*, Portsmouth.' (Spasmodic applause and several muttered variations on the theme of 'who the hell is that then?')

My chances of winning were, of course, non-existent, and quite rightly so. Clive James won and the rest of us were all 'commended' so I have contented myself over the years with the knowledge that I finished joint second with Miss Banks-Smith and a man who went on to become a millionaire several times over by writing the lyrics for *Les Miserables*.

I was lucky to have been there at all. My entry was compiled and posted off by a colleague, Pat Turner, because I considered the very idea of joining in a competition against writers like James a tad presumptuous, and still do. Therefore, I treated the occasion as any self-respecting provincial journalist would - as a day out at my employer's expense - and decided to make the most of it. My main memories are of an occasion where there was too much to drink and too little to eat, a situation which did not commend itself to a teetotaller like me who likes his food. The people from the nationals gathered in pockets of loud conviviality, which got louder and more convivial as the afternoon wore on. I twittered away on the periphery, but to be honest I couldn't wait to get back to Waterloo station and invest in a couple of cheese and pickle rolls.

I also made the mistake of believing that the national Press worked like professional football and that if you performed well in the lower divisions, you would catch the eye of a first division scout and be given a chance in a Fleet Street first team. More than 20 years on I'm still waiting, so either it doesn't work like that, the scouting network is malfunctioning or I'm not as good as I hoped I might be. Either way, it's too late now and though there have been times when the thought of jousting with the best held a powerful appeal, I can't say I'm sorry it never happened. After more than 36 years in the game, I now know what I always suspected - that I am by nature, nurture and instinct a provincial journalist down to my very marrow. Knowing this to be a fact is one thing; trying to explain why is more difficult.

Being born and bred in the Isle of Wight must have something to do with it. It means you are insular from the moment of conception, and being provincial is merely a natural extension of that state. Islanders emerge from the womb with a deep suspicion of all things mainland. My Great Uncle Will once told me that the Isle of Wight was called the Garden Isle because Britain was the dung-heap that nourished it. His disaffection with the rest of the motherland was never properly explained, but he had only ever been to the mainland once and that was to have a medical for the Army which, to his immense relief, he failed. He enjoyed an interesting war as a dispatch rider for the local Home Guard (he was the only one in the village with a motorcycle) and getting inebriated to such a degree that he was once spotted in his back garden wearing his pyjamas and a saucepan on his head taking potshots at passing German bombers with his shotgun.

In that brief foray beyond the Solent he had seen nothing that made him hanker to return and he never did. With that sort of slow-moving blood in my veins, journalism at the most frenetic level was never really an option. But it is only now, after a working life spent in the employ of local newspapers, that I realise people like me actually have as much if not more influence over the lives of our readers than any national newspaper editor. We report on, and rail against, issues that matter directly to our readers, whereas national titles operate on a level so rarefied that the best they can hope to achieve is to influence vague opinion in the stratosphere rather than galvanise direct action on the street.

I remember reading an interview with Paul Newman. Asked who made the important decisions in his household, he replied: "I make all the important decisions, like whether the dollar should be devalued, whether the spending on social services is adequate or whether America should retain its links with NATO.

"Joanne makes all the small decisions like where we live, where the kids go to school, what we have for dinner and so on."

The national newspapers are Paul Newman; the regional titles are Joanne Woodward.

The difference between the provincial and the national Press is not merely confined to pay or perceived position within the communities they serve. It's a difference in the fundamental ethos of the job and it was never more effectively brought home to me than when I was asked to take part in an editors' forum in Chichester cathedral a few years ago chaired by the late Hugh Cudlipp.

He had rounded up several of his pals from the nationals, at least two of whom were knights of the realm. That made me feel a little uncomfortable because I have always regarded an editor with a knighthood as I would a commando with an Iron Cross. It's the wrong honour for the wrong person for all the wrong reasons. Surely editors at every level exist to question the establishment and make life uncomfortable for it? They should never allow their principles to be won over by the promise of preferment. However, it had the makings of an interesting evening and I was plonked at the end of the table as the token hick.

I had tried to warn Cudlipp beforehand that if he took questions from the floor unscreened there was bound to be a parochial inquiry about something to do with my newspaper (the *Chichester Observer*) that would be of no interest to the rest of the panel and of limited interest to most of the audience. He would have none of it. He simply would not accept the fact that faced with a phalanx of some of Fleet Street's most celebrated practitioners anyone could possibly be bothered to discuss anything other than matters of great moment.

His face was a picture when the second question from the floor was posed by a man in a fawn raincoat who sounded like Tam Dalyell. His voice reverberated with suppressed outrage as he began: "Mr Newbery, I wrote to you six weeks ago on the subject of street lighting in the city. Not only did you ignore the existence of my correspondence for two weeks, it actually contained two errors when you finally found space to publish it. What I would like to know is why you..."

And on he went while Cudlipp found several different ways of not catching my eye.

I have wanted to be a journalist for as long as I can remember, and, according to my mother, even longer than that. She can recall me announcing to the family that I wanted to write 'like Peter Wilson' when I was about ten years old. He was then the best-known sports columnist on the *Daily Mirror*, which was then the top-selling newspaper in the country. There is nothing so vaulting as childhood ambition, but my mother took that pronouncement seriously, clinging to it through the years while my career aspirations flitted from policeman, to soldier, to vet, to vicar and back again.

I scrambled through my 11-plus, an achievement which won for me the right to struggle like hell for five years among children at Sandown Grammar School, 90 per cent of whom were far more intelligent than I. I have always believed that Stevie Smith's poem *Not Waving But Drowning* was written to commemorate my years at Sandown where I was academically so far out of my depth that I managed to survive only by keeping one nostril clear of the engulfing tide of essays and equations.

My reward for doing four hours' homework virtually every night (more at weekends) was two O levels - History and English - and deteriorating eyesight from the time spent poring over books deep into the night. The combination of moderate intelligence and a willingness to work hard is a debilitating one. You are led to believe that if you put in the hours you will reap the rewards. It is a flawed philosophy propounded by the likes of golfer Gary Player, who, when someone told him he was a lucky player, is said to have replied: "Yes, and the harder I practise the luckier I get."

What people like Player omit to mention is that you have to have a certain aptitude to begin with. If a modicum of that essential gift is not there, then all the practice in the world won't compensate for its absence. You will end up becoming an accomplished artisan but never a gifted exponent of anything.

But that's not something you want to know when you are young. Peer pressure is a consuming factor, and you strive to be better than them, no matter what the cost. You will even settle for being as good as them at a push, but proving you are no match for them despite all your best efforts is difficult to handle amid all the skin blemishes and insecurities of puberty.

But it was something I had to get used to. You had to get five O levels to graduate to the sixth form, so my paltry two consigned me to a year in the wilderness of what was called '5E.' We were the forgotten tribe; not intelligent enough for advancement but deemed too hard-working not to be given a second chance. We endured a gypsy-like existence, drifting around the campus, deprived of the luxury of a permanent base and regarded with a mixture of sympathy and mild derision. But this exile had its consolations, because we were allowed to sit at the back of any class we fancied, and I always fancied sitting at the back of the fifth-form girls' domestic science class.

There I would perch on a wooden stool, at a table laden with pots and pans and pretend to bend my thoughts to Pythagoras or the progress of Norwegian glaciers, while cocking a constant ear to what was going on at the far end of the room. It also provided the opportunity to chat to the girls at the back of the class, who were as interested in the construction of a peach and walnut flan as I was in the topography of Scandinavia. One day the subject was shellfish, and the teacher had with her an oyster, which was an extraordinarily exotic treat for members of the spam and sausage generation like us. You have to appreciate that this was 1964 on the Isle of Wight, and cockles and mussels were commodities which Molly Malone wheeled in her wheelbarrow through streets broad and narrow. Oysters, as far as we knew, were embryonic pearls. Their libidinous qualities were neither known about nor required when you were 16. Indeed, they could have proved positively terminal to boys like me who were already generating industrial quantities of testosterone.

The teacher held up the opened shell. 'Right,' she said, 'who would like to try this?' A forest of arms shot skywards, one was chosen and its owner stepped forward to further her gastronomic education. She accepted the shell, put it to her mouth and then made the mistake of looking down. There was at least five seconds' silence, before she shrieked 'yeuggghhh, it looks like snot,' whereupon the shell was thrust back in the general direction of the teacher while the girl ran back to her desk holding her apron to her mouth while simultaneously crying and making gagging noises.

The teacher glowered around the room, before settling upon the stricken figure of her guinea-pig. 'Oh don't be so melodramatic Patricia,' she growled, but Patricia was now beyond reproof, having bent herself double and graduated to dry, retching noises.

'Now then,' said the teacher, 'who will eat this lovely oyster?' Not one hand went up, which meant the woman had an uninterrupted view right across to the far side of the room where I sat sniggering.

'Right Newbery,' she said, 'you seem to find this amusing. Perhaps you would care to step forward and give us the benefit of your sophisticated palate.' She knew only too well that no 16-year-old boy is going to back down in a room full of 15-year-old girls, so I strolled forward to my fate, almost being bowled over by Patricia and three of her fluttering friends who were rushing her in the general direction of the toilet with her apron over her head.

The teacher handed me the oyster with a lizard smile, and I forced myself not to look down. I put the shell to my lips, tipped back my head, closed my eyes and swallowed. Unfortunately, anything that looks like sputum usually feels like sputum, and oysters are no exception. It slithered to the back of my mouth and down my throat before I discovered a medical fact with which I had hitherto been unacquainted.

Everyone has a tiny trampoline in their stomach, and the oyster hit mine before rebounding back up through my throat and mouth and back into the shell.

This feat was greeted by a smattering of applause and flushed with triumph I proferred the shell to the teacher.

'Perhaps you would you care for a go now?' I said, smiling sweetly. She gave me a filthy look and three consecutive detentions.

Two evenings a week I left the academic wastelands of 5E and made my way over the railway line, past Sandown railway station and up to the Grove Road residence of one Percy Warder. He was a delightful, almost Dickensian figure, with a warm, gurgly voice like the chap from the Mr Kipling television advertisements. Percy was a retired teacher who, more for the company than the money I suspect, held evening classes for those wishing to master the complexities of shorthand as devised by Isaac Pitman. For a bit extra (though not much) he would also teach you to touch-type and the basics of book-keeping. He was, in effect, a tutor to would-be secretaries, so once again I found myself the only male in the company of at least half a dozen females. I was beginning to realise that being academically inadequate had some advantages.

My mother - still intent upon driving me towards the journalistic career I had first mentioned in passing six or seven years earlier - had the good sense to know that anyone applying for a junior reporter's job was more likely to get it if he had a certificate for 100 wpm shorthand than an O level pass in technical drawing. She had heard about Percy and the two of us made an appointment with him one winter's evening. He welcomed us into his front room, where a coal fire was blazing and a pot of tea was softly steaming. As he sat in his high-backed chair with his chubby face glowing in the flickering firelight and his kind eyes twinkling, he reminded me of Robert Donat in the final scene from *Goodbye Mr Chips*.

Back in the 60s, when boys did woodwork and girls took cookery classes, any reversal of roles was regarded as highly-suspicious. Therefore I represented something of a novelty to Percy. Here was a six-feet four-inch, 17-year-old lad who wanted to learn what, to all intents and purposes, was girls' work on the off-chance that he might get a job working on a newspaper. Percy chuckled as agreement was reached and his smile suggested that he thought he was indulging a misfit's passing fancy. I would almost have agreed with him at the time.

Classes were held in a wooden shed at the end of Percy's garden. Eight of us sat round a rectangular table while the old boy sat at its head dispensing wisdom and producing so much smoke from his pipe that the only relief came in the form of fumes from the paraffin stove in the corner. Health and safety officials would have enjoyed themselves enormously, because it was manifestly neither healthy nor safe. The ozone layer above Percy's house must have been at its thinnest.

In a lean-to tacked on to the back of the shed was where Percy kept his two typewriters, and we dived in there at every opportunity to remind ourselves what oxygen tasted like. I endeavoured to learn touch-typing, but the fact that I am employing just two arthritic forefingers as I clatter out this prose almost 40 years later is testament to the fact that I failed miserably.

I have huge, navvy-like hands that were not made for skittering lightly over the surface of a keyboard and my attempts to do so often drew Percy and his pipe into the tiny annexe.

'Do come and look,' he would invite the rest of the class. 'I keep telling Keith he won't get his work done any faster by depressing two keys with one finger, but I don't think he believes me.'

Then he would chuckle into his pipe and the two girls nearest to him would become covered in a layer of ash and stand there uncomplaining like the calcified remains discovered at the foot of Mount Vesuvius.

Thanks to Percy I mastered the rudiments of shorthand and armed with my certificate for 80 words a minute (a qualification that not even the most academically-endowed student at Sandown Grammar possessed) I strode confidently to the office of Mr Tromans for the 45 seconds of discussion that were to influence the next 45 years of my life.

'Pad' Tromans was a rather fierce little man who had his priorities right. He was surrounded by a lot of clever pupils who had earned the right to attend university in the days before degrees were handed out like drachma at a Greek wedding. Therefore, he had little time to waste on a boy who had been given two chances to pass O levels and still ended up with the two he had managed 12 months earlier. For Mr Tromans it must have felt like being forced to read a limerick in a library full of Shakespeare sonnets.

Little wonder that he gazed at me impatiently over the top of his glasses. 'And what do you intend to do with the rest of your life?' he asked. To his credit, he didn't even pretend to sound interested.

'Well sir, I'd like to be a journalist.'

What passed for a smile flickered across his lips. 'Well... er... er...' (he glanced down at the sheet of paper on his desk) 'Newbery, I have to inform you that only two boys have ever left this school and made a career out of journalism and both were - now how can I put this - considerably better equipped from an academic point of view than you appear to be. I have here leaflets from Lloyds, Barclays and the National Provincial bank. Perhaps you might care to look at them.' He passed them to me without looking up and the discussions as to my future prospects were at an end.

I left Sandown Grammar with few regrets, and returned for the first time 15 years later when I was invited - as editor of one of the Isle of Wight's two weekly newspapers at that time - to be guest speaker at speech day. It was an event I had never been deemed worthy enough to attend as a child, so it would be foolish to deny the sense of self-satisfaction I felt as the serried ranks of bored kids applauded the platform party into the hall. I made the talk as short and unacademic as I could (after all the kids had done nothing to me) and we all trooped out again.

Some of the teachers had lined up to bid us farewell and among them was a man who, as I left the school for the last time 15 years earlier, had waited until I was surrounded by friends before sending me on my way with these encouraging words: "Off you go Newbery. I always said you'd never amount to anything."

Well I hadn't amounted to much, but I had apparently become someone worthy of his attention. As I approached he extended his hand. I stopped, looked at him, looked at his hand, ignored it and walked on. I felt simultaneously ashamed and triumphant. It may have taken 15 years, but now he had some idea of what public humiliation felt like.

The summer of my 17th year was spent playing cricket and working as a stockroom boy in Woolworths, where a scowling Scot of a manager called Jock Murray (whom I came to know and like many years later) did his best to make the three of us work for a living. Among the many accomplishments I mastered during that happy time was the ability to consume an entire strawberry split in the seven seconds it took the lift to descend from the storage area to the shop floor. This was no mean feat, and how it did not come to require the medical extraction of a lolly-stick from a sinus cavity is a small miracle in itself.

My mother could see I was warming to the easy life, and she became wary of her first-born becoming the world's most accomplished Mivvi-masticator. That's why I got home one evening to find her brandishing a copy of Ryde's local newspaper the *Isle of Wight Times*. 'Look,' she said, 'they're advertising for a junior reporter. You've got an interview for the job tomorrow.' Seven days later my career in journalism had begun.

I had grown up with the *Isle of Wight Times*, a little tabloid that on a good week could grow to as many as 12 pages and was greatly prized by its loyal band of readers. It sold around 5,000 copies a week and was produced almost as an after-thought by a printing firm called Lightbowns, whose primary enterprise was the production of technical journals for which it had deservedly earned itself a fine reputation.

The editor of the *Isle of Wight Times* was a chap called Clive Barton who remains to this day one of the most talented journalists I have ever worked with. He could comfortably have graduated to a national newspaper but decided to remain on the Isle of Wight where he indulged his passions for judo and scuba-diving while developing a lucrative sideline supplying the nationals with local stories, many of which were honed and burnished with his own distinctive style. Barton knew how to catch the eye of the news editors on national tabloids, and no pun went unexploited.

He was one of a clutch of experienced old hacks who squatted in various outposts on the Island and augmented their meagre earnings by selling off stories to the nationals, some of which were true. So inventive did some of them become that it was rumoured that the phrase 'it could only happen on the Island' began to be muttered through Fleet Street. That's largely because much of it didn't.

There was one exceptional exponent whose name escapes me. Unfortunately he had died long before I entered the profession so I never got to meet this legend and had to be satisfied with the tales told about him whenever Island journalists chatted among themselves in the tedious phases of various council committee meetings, of which there were plenty.

Just before Christmas one year, this man needed to top up his festive pot and decided that it was about time a freak heatwave - lasting just an afternoon - affected the south-west coast of the Island. He waited for one of those glacial but sunlit winter afternoons and rounded up his wife, kids, picnic basket and beach-ball and this unlikely caravanserai made its way to the nearest beach. Once there, the children donned bathing costumes, the adults set up deckchairs, and the entire family began to frolic in the surf. This came as something of a surprise to passers-by, who were huddled in overcoats and scarves to protect themselves against a temperature that was being driven to below freezing by what has now come to be known as a wind-chill factor.

The enterprising journalist then began to take photographs of his kids playing on the sand. They were obliged to smile through closed mouths as he did so because every time they opened them their breath was immediately converted to steam in the bitter air and was certain to give the game away. The wife was photographed pouring out a pot of cold tea for the same reason.

The journalist then invented a local weather expert who confessed he had never known anything like it. A unique weather phenomenon, caused by the combination of rare trade winds and the jet stream had bathed the south-west coast of the Island in temperatures of 70 degrees Fahrenheit for a few hours only. It was thought to be a record for late November.

The story and photographs were despatched to London, and the following day were featured in five national newspapers. The journalist and his family had a wonderful Christmas and the story passed into Isle of Wight legend.

Barton never went this far, but he never missed an opportunity. I arrived late for work one day, having been up much of the night searching the neighbourhood with my father and our pet Alsatian for a man who had tried to force one of the windows on my sister's bedroom in the early hours. It had been a traumatic time and Barton listened with unaccustomed solicitousness to my story, which appeared word for word in two evening newspapers and the local television news a few hours later.

It was not the last time I was to be Bartonised. In the early hours of one summer night the phone rang at our house. It was Mrs Roberts, the

Bembridge correspondent for the *Isle of Wight Times*, who had been informed that the village's lifeboat had been launched to search for an angler missing from a boat off Ryde.

She thought it might be worth my while popping down to the end of Ryde pier to see what was happening. I drove down through the empty town and asked the chap at the pier gates if he knew of anything going on. He paused mid-sandwich for long enough to say that there had been an ambulance flying around a while ago, but that it had all gone quiet. "You're too late nipper."

I wandered up the deserted pier and gazed out across the sea which was dark and motionless and could barely be heard lapping against the pier. The moon was reflecting on it, the night was balmy and it seemed the least likely place in the world for a tragedy to have befallen anyone. I looked back at the town of Ryde, which was slumped quietly on the side of its hill, and thought that though I had lived in and around the area my entire life, it had never before looked this beautiful.

Suddenly I was aware of footsteps running up the pier towards me. It was a shambling, uncertain stride. Sometimes it stopped and at these moments the silence was filled with an anguished shout. Then the footsteps began again. Eventually the man reached me. His hair was wet and plastered to his head and he seemed to be wearing a jacket that didn't fit.

"Have they found him?" He looked at me when he said it, then wheeled round to gaze out over the sea. "Have they found him?" he shouted again to no-one in particular.

At that time I had been in journalism for less than a year, and two thoughts immediately kicked in. Don't get your notebook out and don't tell him who you are or what you are doing there. In hindsight it seemed callous but it happened for the same reason photographers are able to carry on taking photographs of a disaster rather than dropping their cameras and offering to help. Professional instinct takes over and it seems pointless forsaking your own duties for a futile gesture, no matter how well intentioned.

"Who?" I asked, and it was the only word I was to utter for at least five minutes. The man, obviously distressed, just needed somebody to listen. He told a story so harrowing that even now, more than 35 years after the event, it is carved into my memory. I can recall it in the smallest detail. No note-book was needed.

He and a friend had decided to go fishing for conger eel in a small boat. They were wary because the friend had a particular aversion to these creatures, which are immensely powerful and vicious when cornered. But it seemed like such a serene night and the chances of them landing one were remote anyway. Then the unexpected happened. They hauled in a large specimen and it immediately began to thrash around in the boat. The missing man had begun to edge away and in doing so trapped his foot in the line dangling from the creature's mouth.

The conger managed to throw itself back over the side of the boat taking the man with it. He surfaced and told his friend not to worry. He just had to disentangle the line he said. He disappeared below the sea again and once more seemed calm when he reappeared.

When he came up for the third time he looked at his friend and quietly said: 'Give my love to the kids.' He was dragged under and was never seen alive again. The emergency services had been alerted, and an ambulance had taken the survivor to Ryde hospital. So distraught was the man that he had run from the hospital through the empty, echoing town and back to the seafront, where he unburdened himself to a total stranger in the silence of a late summer night.

I had simply been in the right place at the right time, but I was a novice and the importance and value of the information I had at my disposal did not register. I returned home, got a few hours sleep and began to look forward to the cricket match I was playing in that afternoon. About 11am the forces of Fleet Street fell upon our house and the telephone never stopped ringing for hours. They had learned about the story and discovered I was the only one with the details. Clive Barton was away that weekend, so they asked me to write the copy which would have to be filed in his name as he was their official correspondent.

'Killer conger' screamed the headlines the next day, and the dramatic tale made a page lead in almost every national newspaper. The cheques were sent direct to Barton and he eventually gave me a fiver 'for my help.' Others I spoke to reckon that even back in the sixties he would have been paid hundreds of pounds for the story, which may have explained why he disappeared on diving holidays to the Mediterranean for the next few years. To this day I feel no rancour. If it had not been for Barton I would never have got a break in journalism and never learned so much in such a short time. I was far more upset to discover that the dead man was the cheerful chap who delivered our bread once a week.

In many respects, I got off lightly in my dealings with Clive Barton. He had a lacerating wit, a streak of cynicism that occupied about 90 per cent of his body weight and an admirable lack of respect for everyone, especially those who felt they were entitled to it as of right. Barton never gave it to them as of principle.

It was not easy to warm to him, but it was no problem whatsoever to admire him. We shared the same office for 18 months and I learned more in that time than in the three years of official apprenticeship that were to follow on the evening newspaper in Portsmouth.

Not that Barton actually went out of his way to teach you anything, of course. He didn't have time for things like that. But if you watched and listened, there was plenty to absorb.

The Lightbowns' empire was situated at the bottom of Union Street, about 100 yards from the sea as the gull flies. As you strode down the street you were therefore afforded a stunning view of Spithead - the stretch of sea that separates the Island from the mainland - and the entire length of Ryde Pier which is said to be Britain's second longest and stretches out towards Portsmouth like a half-hearted attempt at reconciliation.

A passenger ferry leaves from there at regular intervals, and the car ferry departs from Fishbourne, which is a few miles along the north-east coast of the Island. The car ferry never attached itself to the end of the pier, which is why I was surprised to see it there one winter's afternoon as I returned to work.

I informed Barton of what I had seen. He cocked a cynical eyebrow and strode out to look for himself. "Mmm, interesting," he muttered as he picked up the telephone receiver and rang a British Rail employee at the end of the pier. The conversation went thus.

"Hello. Clive Barton here, *Isle of Wight Times*. Couldn't help noticing on my way into the office just now that there's a car ferry tied to the end of the pier."

"No there ain't."

"I saw it myself only 20 seconds ago."

"You couldn't have coz it ain't there."

Barton - never one to pursue a pointless conversation - replaced the receiver and dialled the number of the BR manager on the Island. That conversation went thus.

"Hello. Clive Barton here, *Isle of Wight Times*. I've just been talking to one of your idiots at the end of Ryde Pier who seems unable to recognise the fact that a rather large car ferry is tethered no more than 20 yards from the end of his nose."

"Mr Barton, I'd prefer it if you didn't refer to my men as idiots."

"I'd prefer it if you didn't employ idiots, but we all have our crosses to bear."

"Mr Barton, I shall be contacting your employer about this matter!"

"I would if I were you. He has a way with children." End of conversation.

I suspect Clive Barton's Christmas card list got shorter by the year, but you always knew where you stood with him. His speciality was court reporting, and he had the extraordinary ability of being able to sit there all day writing up the previous case while taking notes about the drama unfolding before him. In that way he left court each day with eight or nine stories covered and only one left to write.

One of them involved a young printer at Lightbowns who was renowned for having a full social life and had been arrested for urinating in a public place. Barton, quite rightly, knew the story had to be used. Phil Lightbown, one of the two brothers who were directors of the business, was not so sure and confronted Barton about his reservations.

He shuffled from foot to foot (Barton had that effect on people) before saying: "Now look here mister. That nipper had one or two drinks too many, got caught a bit short and well, you know, had to answer a call of nature. Now that's hardly a crime is it?"

Barton sighed, stopped what he was doing and made a point of slowly flicking back the pages of his notebook until he came to the case in question. "Mr Lightbown, if your idea of 'answering a call of nature' is to stand on one side of Cowes High Street and attempt to aim a stream of urine into a postbox on the other side while announcing to all and sundry your intention to do so, then it is slightly different interpretation to mine."

The story was published the following day.

Barton took a particular delight in savaging the efforts of the repertory company that operated from Ryde Pavilion every summer. He began one review with the words: "There was only one thing wrong with my seat at the Pavilion Theatre last night - it was facing the stage."

He also told me of another opening night when, in his own words 'I turned up and immediately doubled the audience.' About ten minutes into the production an old man arrived and, despite having the choice of about 400 empty seats in the auditorium, chose the one right in the middle of the second row. He clumped his way noisily down the aisle and flipped back every seat in his way until he reached the one he wanted. "The noise," said Barton, "echoed around the empty pavilion like a slow drum-roll in a funeral march."

The old fellow eventually reached his seat and was so exhausted by his exertions that he slumped back heavily in the chair. Unbeknown to him, every seat in the row was attached to the other and 30 chairs immediately collapsed simultaneously and the old boy landed on his back with his feet in the air.

"It was," said Barton, "by far the most amusing performance I had ever seen in the place and it's reckoned to be the only time in the history of the British theatre where the actors stopped what they were doing and applauded the audience."

CHAPTER TWO

Well, the sign did say 'Press'

PRINTERS ARE A distinct type. The pun is not deliberate, but it is unavoidable. The huge majority of the print workers I have known in the past 35 years have been intelligent, frustrated men who in their middle years knew they were capable of more, but realised it was probably too late to bother. I wouldn't go so far as to apply to them the same epigram as that aimed at the miners during the seventies and eighties - that of being lions led by donkeys - but in my experience they usually selected the lesser intellects among them to be their representatives at union level.

This eventually led to their downfall as the power-brokers within the newspaper industry because their leaders couldn't - or wouldn't - see the inevitability of what lay ahead. The skills that so many of their members had honed during lengthy apprenticeships were about to be rendered redundant by the stampede of new technology that was heading in their direction. Kids with computers were able to accomplish in a week what it had taken some trained printers years to master. Their livelihoods were therefore threatened, and with them the hold they had on the newspaper industry.

When I say 'hold,' we are not talking here about a gentle caress of the neck. Their grip was on the testicles of the newspaper proprietors and the slightest squeeze quickly provided them with whatever concession took their fancy. This approach filtered down from national to local level, and as a consequence printers were comparatively well paid throughout the industry. Compared, that is, to journalists. The people who actually generated the material did - and in thousands of cases throughout the country still do - receive a comparative pittance. Back in the mid-sixties the people who processed it were doing very nicely, and this enabled many of them to cloak the intellectual numbness and frustration they were feeling with a good deal of well-upholstered self-satisfaction.

Reasonably bright people with time on their hands usually find some kind of outlet, and with printers it was humour and cynicism. Reporters, especially novices like me, were greeted warily to begin with and whatever peg you may have considered yourself to be on, they couldn't wait to take you down a few levels. It didn't take long for the lads at Lightbowns to put me in my place.

On my third day at work I parked my red Mini in the street outside. In the top left-hand corner of the windscreen was a large sign that said 'Press.' I had spent an hour the previous evening preparing it with ruler and ballpoint with the sole intention of impressing people with my new-found importance. That evening I came out to find a lot of inky fingerprints all over the windscreen.

Furious I went back into the printshop and asked who had done such a thing. About ten hands went up. When I asked why, I was told: "Well, the sign said you wanted people to press it, so we did."

It was a lesson quickly learned, and over the next 18 months I got to know and like the printers at Lightbowns. These were not ordinary men who had little idiosyncrasies, these were idiosyncratic men who, in rare moments of weakness, revealed streaks of ordinariness. They took each other on in mind games to help pass the time, and one tea-break conversation that went down in the annals of Lightbowns concerned two machine-minders, Tony Rumford and Fred Hewison. Fred was a friendly, helpful man; Tony, by his own admission, could be awkward. You were to be flattered if he considered you someone worthy of engaging in an argument.

The conversation on this particular day got round to the subject of the amount of women's underwear that had been disappearing from clothes-lines in the Ryde area.

"Too bloody right," said Fred. "My maid (by which he meant his daughter not his servant) had a brand-new pair of knickers stolen only last night."

"No she didn't," said Rumford without bothering to look up from his sandwich box.

"I'm bloody telling you," said Fred, "that my gal had a brand-new pair of knickers stolen from our line last night."

"No she didn't," said Rumford in that expressionless way guaranteed to infuriate.

Fred duly obliged. "I'm bloody telling you Rumford that my daughter had a brand-new pair of knickers stolen from our clothes-line last night."

Rumford slowly replaced his sandwich. "If they were brand-new, they wouldn't have been on the washing-line would they? For something to be on a washing-line, it has to have been washed. For something to have been washed, it has to have been worn. And if you've worn something it's not brand-new is it."

It was an argument nobody was going to win and one that neither man was prepared to lose. Hours later, above the clatter of their adjacent flatbed presses, they were still snarling their weird logic at each other.

I first met one of the co-owners of the company - Phil Lightbown - without realising it. On the first Wednesday press night I wandered out into the printworks to be confronted by a slim, smiling man with a shiny face. He was dressed in overalls, was brandishing a large spanner and looked for all the world like a caretaker or a mechanic.

"How's it going young man?" he asked.

"Not so bad mate," I replied, and moved on. Mick Bull, who was to become a friend and remains so to this day, sidled over. "You know who that is don't you?" Encouraged by my blank look, he added: "That's Phil Lightbown. He's the boss."

A couple of minutes later the boss's wife came bowling through, and there was no doubting her place in the hierarchy. A stocky, doughty woman she was regarded warily by the men. It was obvious that here was a woman with whom liberties were taken at one's peril. Behind her back, the lads referred to Eileen Lightbown as ''Er' and like many nicknames this one was born out of a mixture of fear and respect. She always hustled and bustled around the place, as if you had just caught her in the middle of doing something far more important.

"What shall we do about this?" somebody would ask. "Better ask 'Er," would come the immediate reply. Though Mrs L could be brusque, she was unfailingly civil and imbued with an innate sense of fairness that would have made her an excellent magistrate. She and Phil were an ideal fit and I got to know and like them both over the years. But as a young reporter, there were times when I had cause to doubt their commitment to my complete comfort at work.

'Er's mother, Mrs Hendon, lived above the office Barton and I shared and every Monday she did her washing. If it was raining, the washing was hung up to dry on makeshift lines strung across the office. Many was the time we turned up for work to find ourselves operating in a makeshift laundrette, and muffled conversations had to be conducted through lines of damp petticoats and pillow-cases. Indeed, Barton once swore that he had been sitting there issuing instructions to me without realising that I had left for lunch five minutes earlier.

'Er's mum assumed mythical proportions to me. Though intimately acquainted with her nether garments, I can never recall meeting the lady herself in the 18 months I spent on the *Isle of Wight Times*. She was the source of one or two sharp exchanges between Barton and Mrs L which he invariably lost because she was not the type to acknowledge, or even notice, his subtle point-making.

"But Mrs L," he would implore, "conducting a conversation with the town clerk is rendered infinitely more difficult by having a soggy tea-towel flapping around one's ears."

"The washing stays," 'Er would reply, and go stomping upstairs to enjoy a cup of tea with her mother. Barton would look at me, roll his eyes, gather up his notebooks and set off for another lucrative day at court. I would find a drip-dry spot and set about learning my trade by typing out the tide tables and the chemists' rota.

At every opportunity I would dart out the back to the printworks and watch mesmerised by the intricacies of the linotype machines. They were exquisite pieces of machinery which, in the hands of experts like George Pritty, Jack Scovell and Mac Richards, could transform my humdrum efforts into slugs of type. These linotypes were, though we didn't realise it at the time, environmentally friendly in a smelly, unhealthy sort of way. All the type, once used, was melted down and recycled and I used to console myself with the knowledge that the very molten lead that was transformed that week into my two paragraphs on the Christian Union had, only weeks before, been proclaiming the latest council extravagances on the front page. There was pride by association in things like that when you were a young reporter.

George Pritty - a bluff, loud and affable man - was stricken by a form of narcolepsy which meant that he had a tendency to fall asleep in the middle of setting a piece of copy. It was unnerving to see George slumped over his keyboard sound asleep, while the rest of the workforce went noisily about their business.

Jack Scovell was just the opposite. A small, spry man, he kept forgetting that the ledge of the linotype machine overhung his seat. Almost every day it seemed, he would leap up at some point and bang his forehead on its brass casing, which meant that he was rarely seen without a large plaster just above his left eyebrow. Jack was also an expert equestrian, and when his workload eased he would tap out columns of self-generated copy on local gymkhanas which got gratefully absorbed into the sports pages of the paper.

Mac Richards would do the same with cricket. His name was synonymous with the sport on the Isle of Wight and some of his match reports were minor masterpieces of wit and percipience. He was a man who believed that cricket matches were to be enjoyed, not necessarily won. It was not just skill he sought in its exponents, but character. Players Mac liked, or who made him laugh, were selected for his special representative sides, and I am proud of the fact that for many years I was chosen to play for his Mallyshags XI. For many seasons we were officially credited by the *Cricketer* magazine as playing in the last competitive match in Britain every season.

Mallyshags is an old Isle of Wight word for 'caterpillars that are slow in the field' (a typical Mac touch) and when you are playing towards the end of October (no matter what the weather) swaddled in jumpers and thermal undergarments, spring-heeled and nimble you most conspicuously are not. There were moments during these matches when Mac would literally clutch himself with glee and you could hear him giggling helplessly on the boundary.

If he needed umpires for these matches he would purposely ask men suffering from gout or in the throes of recovering from a hernia operation. Anything to make them feel perverse or unsympathetic, and he always got his man because nobody ever turned him down.

The man to whom even Mac deferred in the eccentricity stakes at Lightbowns was Bill Sievwright, a former sailor with an unflappable approach to life and a sense of humour for which the word droll had been invented. Bill looked a bit like Peter Lorre and he always had a half-smile on his face, as though he had just heard a good joke and was savouring it for a while before deciding whether to pass it on.

On other occasions, when it was time for a tea-break, he would shout: "Come on my lads. Time to pick up your parrots and make for the ship." I later discovered that this was the favourite cry of a petty officer with whom Bill served and it was originally employed to usher along sailors who were serving in exotic parts and who thought it would be a good idea to arrive back in good old blighty with an example of the local bird-life

Bill's perfect foil was Eric White, a thin, jittery man who chain-smoked and whose life everyone knew would one day be curtailed by the deadly combination of too much adrenalin and nicotine. I once saw Eric hover outside a lavatory and, quite literally walk away and come back to the door three times before saying to nobody in particular: "Nah. I'll have a piss later. I must get this done."

Bill and Eric were mates for the simple reason that though totally different in both design and attitude, they had one thing in common. Both were decent, genuine men who recognised these qualities in each other. Nine years after I left Lightbowns, I was reunited with them when I was asked to become editor of a new newspaper called the *Isle of Wight Weekly Post*. It was being produced on the same antiquated machinery and the only way we could be sure of getting a newspaper out was to stay all day and night to print, collate and fold it. Bill and Eric were among the chain-gang, and I must be one of the few editors ever to write, sub-edit, help print, stack and deliver his newspaper.

One morning at about 3am, Eric was the only one there still printing the individual sheets, Bill was the only one there still collecting them up to be placed in the folding machine and I was the only one there ready to stack the completed newspapers out the back. As the night got longer, Eric's patience got shorter. Bill, meanwhile, was stoically going about his business, whistling or humming as he did so.

Eventually Eric could stand it no longer. He turned up the speed of his machine which had the effect only of creasing the individual sheets. Eventually Bill could stand it no longer either.

"Eric old son," he said in that calm and measured way of his, "if you're going to fold these papers as well as print them I might as well piss off home."

Nothing ever seemed to annoy Bill Sievwright and his patience was legendary. It meant that those of a less tolerant disposition were only too happy to give him the more demanding jobs - and they didn't come any more demanding than looking after the apprentices. I once saw him attempting to pass on the secrets of basic book-binding to one young lad, who was congenitally unco-ordinated. His fingers flapped and clacked like clothes pegs, and try as he might every attempt at binding pages ended up looking like a parcel of fish and chips. Bill smiled and persisted. 'No Barry, try it again like this.'

Three times Barry tried and three times he failed. Bill merely smiled around the room and said to nobody in particular and everybody in general; "Christ. It makes you wish you ate your young..."

Bill, Jack, George, Mac, Eric, Phil and Eileen. They're all dead now but if I close my eyes I can see them all in a shifting, mingling, laughing, shouting, groaning, clanking, clattering pastiche among the noise and grime of that small print-works. The clarity of that memory, and the fact that it has remained with me for so many years, must surely be the definitive test of how important a role some people play in your life, though you may not realise it at the time.

CHAPTER THREE

Mr Palmer, you're out of order!

IN MY EXPERIENCE, most councils are where idealists, the prematurely retired, the terminally nosey and the self-important go to get the inside track. They hope it will give them status and influence in the community; they normally end up seeking care in the community. Councillors are like football referees; they volunteer to be abused for doing something they hope will help others.

The relationship between newspapers and politicians - both local and national - has been described as being similar to that between a dog and a lamp-post. This may be colourful, but it's not strictly true. However (and I can talk only from a provincial perspective) it is the duty of an editor to scrutinise the actions of local authorities, and to give readers every opportunity to express their concerns. Where else are they to go if they feel they have been treated unfairly or have strong feelings they wish to express against a particular policy?

For that reason I have never gone out of my way to develop any sort of relationship with councillors or council officers. It has never been a personal issue and probably I have deprived myself of some rewarding friendships over the years, but local democracy can only properly be served by an editor and a local authority that maintain a respectful distance from each other. When both become part of the same establishment, human nature dictates that the truth is bound to suffer or, at the very least, become distorted. It is, after all, far more difficult to carry uncomplimentary stories or write critical editorials about people with whom you had dinner only the week before. It is better, therefore, not to leave oneself open to such temptation.

It is the same with MPs. I have made a point of never meeting any serving MPs in constituencies covered by any of the newspapers I have edited. This is not a view shared by many of my fellow editors, but it has always worked for me.

MPs need local editors far more than we need them. If a story breaks that is destined to show them in a favourable light, they or their secretary or agent will soon be on the phone to provide chapter and verse, so you have no worries on that score. If, however, a story breaks that may make life awkward for them, you can be sure that they will make life awkward for you.

Therefore an editor has absolutely nothing to gain by seeking to cultivate their friendship or confidence.

Covering council meetings for a newspaper can be a grim business, and it is only now that I realise the first council meeting I ever covered as a junior reporter was also the most entertaining. It has all been downhill since that March evening in 1966 when I turned up for a meeting of Bembridge Parish Council that was held in the room above the fire station.

So naive was I in the ways of the municipal world that I began to take down a note of the previous month's minutes that were being read by the clerk at the start of the meeting. Only a kindly intervention from John Winter, a more experienced hand from the *County Press*, stopped me from scribbling my way into a lather. He said I should just sit back and relax because something would crop up. It always did at Bembridge, he said.

Sure enough, no sooner had the feeling returned to my writing hand than the Saga of the Hedge began to unfold. Months before, the council had written to a householder in the village and asked him to trim his hedge because it was encroaching on the village playing-field which bordered his property. The man wrote back and said that if the council wanted the hedge cut they were the best people to do it because it did not belong to him. The council replied in a slightly firmer tone, repeating their request and assuring the householder it was indeed his hedge, not theirs, so would he please get on with cutting it.

The man replied, stating that he had consulted his deeds which confirmed what he had known all along, to wit, that he had no responsibility for the hedge whatsoever and under no circumstances would he undertake to cut it or pay for the work to be carried out.

This was about three or four months into the dispute and by this time the privet in question was threatening to overrun the eastern seaboard of the Isle of Wight. The council replied once more, demanding that the hedge be cut without delay and threatening everything short of deportation, castration and excommunication should the task not be carried out to their satisfaction.

On the evening I turned up, the council had received the latest missive from its indignant ratepayer, and members were poised on the edge of their seats as the clerk began to read: "Dear Sirs, further to our correspondence regarding the hedge on the boundary of my property and the village playing-field. I am now in a position to assure you without fear of contradiction that said hedge did indeed belong to you. I burned it down last night and the roots were definitely on your side. Yours faithfully..."

Amid much harrumphing and outraged gasps from the table to our left, I looked across at John Winter, who picked up his pen and he gave me an 'I told you so' smile.

Bembridge Parish Council had attained legendary status among reporters on the Island, and the old hands on the reporters' table were eager to regale new boys like me with some of the more unusual exploits. One concerned the council's investment in the latest fire-fighting technology around the start of the 20th century. It consisted of a hand-cart which, instead of being loaded with buckets and pulled to the blaze by a bunch of village lads, had been fitted with a stirrup pump. The council was justifiably proud of its investment in new technology, and one particular member, a Councillor Palmer, was instructed to stop whatever he was doing the next time the alarm bell sounded, dash to the blaze and report back on how the new pump had performed.

Unfortunately, Mr Palmer was by some years the oldest member of the council, and when the alarm rang out right in the middle of a council meeting he creaked slowly to his feet and shuffled out of the door to fulfil his appointed task. The meeting was still in progress when he returned an hour later, and he slumped on the table in front of him gasping for breath.

"Well Councillor Palmer," demanded the chairman, "How did our new pump perform?"

"Gentlemen," said the old boy, "it was pitiful. I could have pissed twice as high."

"Councillor Palmer," cried the chairman, "you are out of order!"

"I know," said the old boy, "otherwise I could have pissed five times as high."

This story was told to me by Fred Kingswell, a *County Press* reporter who looked as though he had been born at the age of about 52 and had never altered. He reminded me in many ways of Mr Godfrey, the gentle old pacifist in *Dad's Army*. He lived with his sister, never had a bad word to say about anyone and as a consequence nobody ever had a bad word to say about him. Imagine the mortfication he felt, then, on being branded an uncaring glutton in front of the massed ranks of the Isle of Wight women's institutes.

Fred had been sent to cover the federation's annual meeting and found himself seated at a table for four, on which, naturally enough, was piled a delightful home-made tea for the same number of people. Come the appointed hour, and Fred began to work his way through the scones and fairy cakes. The minutes passed and nobody came to join him, so Fred munched on figuring that it would be an act of consummate rudeness to waste such a spread. Eventually he scoffed the lot and, on saying his goodbyes, returned to the office to write up the day's events.

As so often happens in local newspapers, the report was never published. It could have been lack of space, lack of interest or a lack of willingness on the part of the editor to devote several columns to what in those days were details of bland domesticity. The one person entirely blameless in the affair was Fred, who had carried out his duties to the letter.

The following year he returned to cover the event once again and settled back while the president went about outlining the details of the day. As the sun filtered into the warm, dusty hall Fred's eyelids began to droop and he was drifting into that delicious limbo-land between indifference and vague attention when the phrase 'appalling lack of coverage last year' fell upon his ears like a bucket of iced water. He returned to his senses just in time to see the president point her pudgy arm in his direction. It was followed by 200 pairs of vengeful eyes.

"And there's the man," said the president, her voice swooping and shrieking like a lost gull, "who last year ate enough food for four people and never wrote a word!" Thus was the most harmless, inoffensive, likeable man in the Isle of Wight branded forever as the gluttonous bete noir of the Isle of Wight's menopausal legions.

I spent many a dreary night with Fred huddled in a dim corner of Ryde Town Hall, where we were perfectly positioned to witness mild antipathy between councillors develop over the years into deep-seated feuds that were based not on politics (most of them were 'Independents' anyway) but on class differences. One of the most virulent existed between Alderman Ramage and Councillor 'Black' Jack Brazier. Ramage owned a local chemist's shop; Brazier was a railwayman and a former union activist. Ramage purred and persuaded; Brazier snapped and barked. Take it from me, opposites do not attract in a council chamber. Most come to loathe one another.

The issue that brought this particular schism to a head was whether or not fluoride should be introduced into the local water supply. Ramage gave a considered opinion, based on the not inconsiderable knowledge he had acquired during more than 30 years as a pharmacist. Fred drew my attention to the fact that Brazier was beginning to shuffle in his seat and glance around the chamber to catch the eye of anyone who shared his simmering disaffection with what was being said. Other councillors - who knew the genesis of a Brazier eruption when they saw one - suddenly affected to have a deep interest in their minutes or the flaking stucco on the chamber ceiling.

Ramage hummed along until the point came when Brazier could take no more. He leapt to his feet and bellowed: "Mr chairman! I'm not going to sit here and take the word of a petty pill-peddler and purveyor of toilet rolls! I shall adjourn to the corridor for a fag!" So saying, he turned on his heel and stomped out of the room.

Ramage kept talking as though nothing had happened. Indeed, so immersed was he in the technical side of the discussion, that he was probably unaware that anything had.

Two of the most high-profile Island councillors over the past 30 years were Jeff Manners and Morris Barton, whom I first met when they were employed as printers at the *County Press*. Manners was a florid, strident, stocky little man with a loud voice and politics that were not entirely incompatible with his fondness for the music of Wagner. Barton was a thin, saturnine, quietly-spoken individual with a slightly sinister, implacable belief in socialism. He reminded me in many ways of Harold Wilson's former mouthpiece, Joe Haines.

Manners and Barton would enliven many an afternoon in the pressroom, jabbing fingers in the general direction of each other and occasionally allowing their disagreements to descend into personal abuse. 'Bloody commie' and 'nasty little Nazi' were among the endearments that sometimes ricocheted around the room as the exchanges became fraught.

It therefore came as something of a surprise to see them both serving as Liberal councillors a few years later. Even the Liberal Party's reputation for embracing a broad church of political opinion was severely tested by these unlikely recruits, but for a variety of reasons it provided a convenient stop-over point for both men. Of the two, Barton was far more comfortable with the policies of his adopted party, whereas Manners found much of it anathema.

He was probably the only member of the Liberal Party in the country who, when asked his views on nuclear disarmament, was on record as offering his back garden for the deployment of rocket silos. It came as no surprise when he eventually became an 'independent Liberal,' which provided him with the freedom to lash out at all and sundry on any topic that took his fancy. He did it with massive amounts of venom, no little humour and (most worryingly of all as far as some people were concerned) shafts of common-sense. He kept getting re-elected anyway.

Manners was not a man for whom the word compromise held much appeal. He preferred the direct approach to solve any problem, and his other claim to fame on the Island was that of being the only football referee to send off both teams in the same match.

While editing the *Weekly Post* in the 70s, I was approached by a man who felt the paper needed to be spiced up with a diary column chronicling the idiosyncrasies and foibles of some councillors. We decided to give it a go, and Moleman made his first appearance. He succeeded in making local government interesting and amusing, and some of the councillors - Manners among them - were delighted whenever they featured in his musings.

Others, however, did not take so kindly to being mocked, and I recall at least two solicitors' letters threatening all sorts of dire consequences should we continue to feature their client in this way. We did, and there weren't.

Small-town solicitors often make the mistake of thinking that small-town editors are there for the taking. They don't seem to realise that we are trained to know just how far we can go and are therefore not intimidated by embossed letterheads and threats couched in Latin. One actually sent me a letter threatening to sue if I didn't apologise for featuring his client's court case in the previous week's newspaper, claiming that it had been an invasion of privacy. I replied by telling him to stop wasting my time and his client's money - and copied the letter to the client.

Most solicitors' letters are signed with an arrogant little squiggle that bears no resemblance to the name of the person or company from whom it has been sent. Whenever I reply, I replicate the squiggle on the envelope and don't put the reference number at the top of the letter. Silly I know, but deeply satisfying. Who do they think they are anyway?

I once read that Neil Kinnock had a most effective way of replying to abusive letters. If the sender actually had the courage to include their name and address (they usually don't) he would return the missive with a note saying simply: "Dear Mr Smith, I think you should be told that some idiot is sending me abusive letters and using your name and address." I've used that technique a couple of times and heartily recommend it.

Anyway, back to Moleman. He kept jibing away and it was obvious he was well-informed. There was a huge debate on the Island as to who the spy could be, and my name was usually mentioned together with a lad called Michael Merritt who was one of our trainee reporters. We were both flattered by the association, and often did what we could to send people off in pursuit of false trails. But the true identity has remained a secret for 25 years, and if people knew who it was they would be astonished.

When he arrived on the *Weekly Post* as a kid, Merritt was a gauche enthusiast who nevertheless had two of the qualities needed by anyone seeking to make their way in journalism - a keen news sense and a thick skin. The last I heard he was working in London contributing regularly to Nigel Dempster's diary column in the *Daily Mail* and hob-nobbing with Frances Shand-Kydd, Princess Diana's mother.

It is a far cry from the young man who once fell down the County Hall steps in Newport with a choc-ice in his pocket, and was reprimanded by a judge in the crown court for sitting in the press box with his feet up reading a copy of the *Daily Mirror*.

CHAPTER FOUR

Savile, Stonehouse and a letter from Mountbatten

THOSE WHO ARE chosen to skim over the high seas of journalism meet the great and the good as a matter of course. But even those of us who paddle in the stagnant backwaters are required to meet a selection of egos at close quarters, whether we want to or not. In my experience, the eagerness with which these encounters are anticipated usually varies with age. The younger you are, the brighter the stars in your eyes.

My first celebrity interview was with Jimmy Savile in about 1968, when for reasons that escape me now he spent a day at a holiday camp on the Island. The generation that recalls Savile merely as the bespangled host of *Jim'll Fix It* and the shell-suited shuffler from countless marathons will find it difficult to appreciate just how high his profile was in the sixties. He was the first-ever host of *Top of the Pops* at a time when those who presented the show (David Jacobs, Pete Murray and Alan Freeman) were all old enough to be the fathers of those who actually watched it. Savile was in the same age-range, but he did his best not to make the fact obvious. He had invented his own language and his own outfits and recognised the importance of the word 'image' when most people thought it was simply another word for a photograph. In the vernacular of the day, he was considered 'hip.'

We met in the holiday camp bar at about 9am, and there in the forlorn surroundings of brimming ashtrays, half-empty beer glasses and the stale stench of the previous night's jollifications, we spoke. I was a little disappointed that he did not greet me with the immortal words "Now then! Now then! Howzabout we 'ave ourselves a little discussion young man!" but I was soon to discover that little about Savile in private is what you get to see in public.

He wasn't rude or high-handed; far from it. He was friendly in a remote and wary sort of way, and after talking to him for about 20 minutes I realised he had spoken a great deal but had said very little. I knew as much about him when we parted as I had when we met, and not for the first time in my career I had been fended off by a professional. Well over 25 years later I was not in the least surprised to hear Professor Anthony Clare say that of all the people he had interviewed for his Radio Four programme *In the Psychiatrist's Chair*, Savile had been the only one on whom he had not been able to make the slightest impression.

He found, as I did, that Savile is surrounded by a thin, invisible but totally impenetrable shield behind which he shimmers but remains a secret.

A couple of years ago, Louis Theroux made a documentary in which he accompanied Savile for a few weeks. Not surprisingly, Savile was a mass of contradictions - gregarious but lonely; altruistic but selfish; publicly open but privately closed. He had four homes dotted throughout the country, but nothing in the fridge in any of them. His late mother's bedroom was maintained in pristine condition, and her wardrobe of clothes was dry-cleaned at regular intervals, despite the fact that she had been dead for more than 20 years. When Savile was booked into a hotel together with Theroux and the rest of the crew during a visit to Scotland, he chose to sleep alone in the camper van outside.

The one thing about Savile that probably has never changed is his autograph. In the extravagant loop of the J he drew a smiley face, and in his surname the S was a dollar sign and the L a pound sign. My simplistic interpretation was that it betrayed within the man a willingness to be happy if there was money involved, and when I mentioned this fact in one of my weekly columns a few years ago it drew an immediate response from one reader.

He wrote to say that he had gone to school with Jimmy Savile and was annoyed by the fact that he had always maintained he began his working life in the pit, and implied that it was a noble calling from which he had worked long and hard to escape to better things. 'He had no choice,' said my correspondent. 'He was a Bevin Boy.' These were young men who were conscripted into the mining industry in the last two years of the second world war, thereby avoiding the necessity of having to serve in the armed forces.

The writer went on to say that he had contacted Savile a few years earlier, and reminded him of their shared heritage and the fact that their respective families had been brought up in the same street, in the hope that he would agree to help with a charity with which he (the writer) was heavily involved.

The reply from the man who had been knighted by both the Pope and the Queen for his charitable work was brief and to the point. 'You couldn't afford me,' he wrote.

The one time you can be certain that the gods will be only too willing to descend from Mount Olympus and associate with provincial hacks is when they have a book to promote. Nothing is too much trouble. They will put themselves out to visit you, especially those whose best days are considered to be behind them.

The vagaries of a career in the public spotlight were brought home to me while I was working for *The News* at Portsmouth in the eighties. Two people - one a man the other a woman - came calling with a book to push. Had the interviews taken place ten years earlier, the man would not have been able to fight his way through the throng of Press photographers from throughout the world, and the woman would have been surrounded by a crowd aiming autograph books and saucy remarks in her general direction.

But when I interviewed them, both progressed unacknowledged and virtually unrecognised past dozens of staff at the newspaper's head office.

The man turned up on time in reception. "There's a Mr Stonehouse downstairs to see you," I was informed. A couple of minutes later, one of the most famous fugitives in British political history came walking slowly along the corridor. John Stonehouse, the former Walsall MP who had faked his own drowning and was eventually sentenced to seven years for fraud, theft and deception, looked like a retired geography master. He had a fey, apologetic smile, and clothes that betrayed a shabby gentility. Like the man himself, they had seen better days.

Stonehouse had written his first novel, and was on the promotional treadmill. He answered my questions with polite weariness and halfway through our conversation I asked if he would like some coffee. Indeed he would, though his enthusiasm palled when it arrived in plastic cups from the nearby machine.

He was sorry to be a frightful bore, he said, but did I by any chance have a china cup handy and would I mind awfully if he poured the coffee into it? He clearly felt an explanation was necessary. "Even in prison," he said quietly, "we managed to avoid plastic cups."

What Stonehouse did not manage to avoid, however, was the company of the most reviled man in Britain. While serving his time in Wormwood Scrubs, he played Moors murderer Ian Brady in the final of the prison chess championships. And lost.

Like most people who have spent years in public life, Stonehouse had an ability (almost an eagerness) to laugh at himself. It's often a defensive technique that reveals more about the person than they realise, but in Stonehouse's case the amusement seemed genuine when he told me how disappointed the Australian police were when they realised the identity of the man they took into custody on Christmas Eve 1974.

"I had fondly believed," said Stonehouse, "that I was the most famous fugitive in the world and that my capture was something of a coup for them. But for one blissful moment, they actually believed they had caught Lord Lucan. I have to say, their disappointment was manifest."

Barbara Windsor's career has often been described as mercurial, and I got to interview her during one of the down periods. The *Carry On* films were a distant memory and *EastEnders* was not even on the horizon. She was making a living from appearances on television game shows like *Give Us a Clue*, pantomimes and taking second-rate plays around the provinces.

She had been advised to write an autobiography, and though it was interesting to members of my generation, it was hardly leaving scorch marks on the bookshelves as people snatched it away.

But Windsor was the epitome of a trouper. She called me 'darlin' in that unaffectionate way she has, smiled on cue, reeled off the anecdotes and displayed that indefatigable optimism that is common to most show business types I have met. When I asked her whether she was contemplating retirement, she replied: "And live on what darlin'?" Then she paused, and said: "The great thing about this game is that you never know what's round the corner. There's a bit of life in the old girl yet." She cackled the Windsor cackle and seemed genuinely relieved when somebody from our finance department sidled up to ask for an autograph. You got the impression that Barbara Windsor could tolerate losing anything in life except the pleasure of being recognised. She has grasped the *EastEnders*' lifeline and shows no signs of letting go. No whines about the workload. No complaints about intrusions into privacy. Like I said, an admirable trouper who deserves everything that comes her way.

The most unprepossessing author I interviewed was someone I had never heard of who was eagerly promoting a book whose name I had forgotten the day after we met. But this man was a working journalist, and they are a delight to interview because they know precisely what you are looking for. Therefore, we got the preliminaries over in no time at all and sat down to have a natter about the industry.

Just before he left, I asked if he had anything else in the pipeline. He paused and smiled. "Well," he said. "I'm working on something at the moment and if it comes off it will be one of the best-selling books of recent years." I must have looked a little dubious. "But we always say that don't we?"

As he turned to leave I asked if he could tell me what it was about. "I wish I could, but I can't," he said. "But don't worry, if it comes off you'll hear about it all right." His name was Andrew Morton and the something he was working on was *Diana: Her True Story*.

Diana was one of the few members of the Royal family I ever wanted to meet, for reasons that had more to do with lust than loyalty. The closest I came was shaking hands with Prince Charles when he made a visit to the Isle of Wight. It was about 1982 or 1983, and in an attempt to be polite and make the required small talk I said that it was a pity his wife had not been able to join him. I realise now I must have been about the 500th person to say the same thing that day, yet he still managed a faintly stoical smile before moving along to the next inevitable inquiry after his wife's health.

It was clear from watching the prince that day that the one art from which he derives little pleasure is that of communication. He is awkward in company and goes in for a lot of hand gestures and unnatural grinning. His sister - Princess Anne - is quite different.

I met her at an awards lunch in London, and it fell to her to hand me a lump of perspex as a reward for some sports writing I had been doing. The first thing I noticed was her firm handshake. The second was her flirty blue eyes.

"And what sports have you been writing about?" she asked.

"Anything that doesn't involve horses, I'm afraid."

"And why would that be?"

"Because they frighten me to death to be perfectly honest."

"Well you need to become familiar with them. We must see what we can do about that won't we," she chuckled, and flashed the familiar lop-sided smirk. I thought it went well under the circumstances, but I'm still awaiting the royal summons to Gatcombe Park.

Lord Mountbatten of Burma was a regular visitor to the Isle of Wight, where he was Governor. He seemed to take his duties pretty seriously and was always opening a playground ('do you chaps really want me to pose on this children's slide - oh all right then') or hosting the royal visit to Cowes Week, where he often seemed to spot the picture opportunities before the photographers. No sooner had they finished fiddling with their lens than those regal features came shimmering into focus.

He also provided me with the ultimate example of name-dropping. During the Queen's silver jubilee in 1977, he was due to be principal guest at a special gala show in the old theatre on Sandown Pier. The *Weekly Post*, of which I was editor at the time, carried a huge advertisement for the event. Right in the middle, in the biggest, boldest typeface, were the words 'TO BE HELD IN THE PRESENCE OF THE EARLY MOUNTBATTEN OF BURMA.'

The EARLY Mountbatten of Burma! If I could have got my hands on the guilty typesetter at that precise moment, the following week's front-page headline would have read 'Editor pleads guilty to murder through diminished responsibility.'

I decided to get my apology in before he realised there was anything to apologise for. I cut out the offending ad, and sent it to his home at Broadlands with a covering note that apologised for the error and added that 'at least it is better for you to be the Early Mountbatten of Burma rather than the Late Mountbatten of Burma.' It was a clever-dick comment that was to sound horribly hollow two years later when the old boy was blown to bits by the IRA off the coast of Ireland, but at the time it was intended to take the steam out of the situation.

About a week later this reply arrived. It read:

'Dear Mr Newbery,

Thank you for sending me your cutting with the amusing misprint.

I showed your letter to the Queen and Prince Philip and they particularly liked your remark about it is better for me to be 'early' than 'late.'

It may amuse you to know that when I gave the principal address at a meeting of the India Association of Great Britain in Manchester, the Chairman, Dr Pandey, met me in great excitement and said that his wife had just given birth to a baby daughter and he intended to call her after me if I would give my permission.

I asked what name he was going to give her and he told me "Early" so he was ahead of you in choosing this name for me.

Yours sincerely

Mountbatten of Burma.'

I am not, by instinct, a collector. Memorabilia always gets chucked into the loft, but I had that letter framed. It achieved a particular poignancy two years later when Mountbatten was assassinated but the letter is also a perfect example of Mountbatten's common touch. He knew when he wrote it that by including the ultimate piece of name-dropping ("I showed your letter to the Queen and Prince Philip...") he was ensuring maximum exposure.

I have never met the Queen and indeed turned down an opportunity to do so during her golden jubilee year. Together with about 1,200 other editors, I received an invitation to join Her Majesty and Prince Philip for a reception at Windsor Palace, and would I be kind enough to confirm my acceptance to The Master of the Household. At that time, the success of the jubilee was by no means certain, and I remain convinced this shindig was organised as part of an affection offensive to win the support of the Press.

As I mentioned earlier, in more than 25 years of being a local newspaper editor, I have deliberately avoided meeting any local MP or council leader socially, and have always politely refused invitations to lunch. It has never been anything personal, simply a conviction that at some time or other I was going to carry something critical of them in my newspaper, and I didn't want my impartiality to be compromised by friendship or even acquaintance. Local democracy is better served if editors and politicians - local and national - keep each other at arm's length.

Though it seemed unlikely the Queen was going to tap me up for a favour, I felt instinctively that we were all being used; that the glitter of royalty was deemed irresistible and was being employed to win us over. Consequently, I was one of a handful to turn down the invitation. *The Daily Mail's* renowned columnist Linda Lee-Potter was another. I don't think either of us have anything against the monarchy, but that particular convocation didn't seem right then and it doesn't now. I have no regrets whatsoever, though my family were less than impressed and regarded my action as treasonable.

My attendance, however, was clearly taken for granted. A colleague who did go along showed me the official programme in which all the attendees were listed - and there was my name along with the rest of them. He said he only just managed to catch a distant glimpse of the royal perm as it was whisked straight towards Fleet Street's finest, who swarmed all over the poor woman, squirming like maggots in a hot light. The most ingratiating, apparently, were the representatives from those newspapers like the *Independent* and the *Guardian*, who are less well-disposed towards the monarchy as a matter of what they like to think of as 'principle.' Sophisticated though they consider themselves to be, these people were little better than a bunch of pre-pubescent girls wimpering and sighing over secret objects of desire.

Of all the well-known people I've met over the years, there were only two I didn't particularly like - Derek Hatton and Jimmy Greaves. The former came as no surprise, the latter did.

Hatton was the deputy chairman of Liverpool council at the time (did anyone ever know who the chairman was?) and his sweaty, pouty face was everywhere. The extreme left-wing policies he and his cohorts espoused brought Liverpool to its knees, but it provided Hatton with an opportunity to linger where he loved to be - in the spotlight. He was known not to refuse any opportunity to be filmed, photographed or quoted, so when I heard he was going to appear on a televised chat-show in Southampton I requested an interview via one of the station's press officers. Her name was Zoe McIntyre, who had been one of my trainee reporters on the *IW Weekly Post* about ten years earlier. She arranged for Hatton and me to meet, somewhat incongruously, in the lounge of a select hotel in genteel Bexhill-on-Sea.

I arrived on time. Hatton didn't. He eventually turned up about an hour late in a manner expected of a socialist and self-styled man of the people - in an expensive suit with his driver in tow. He glanced over to where we were standing, but there was no hint of an apology. "I'm gonna freshen up," he said, and swept up the stairs leaving his driver to bring the luggage.

About half an hour later he sauntered back down. In the meantime, my mood had not improved. "You fresh enough now?" I inquired.

We both decided to forgo little civilities like a handshake, and made our way to a public room in which Zoe had arranged for a corner to be curtained off. There followed a short, frank and invigorating exchange during which expressions of mutual antipathy were freely exchanged. Hatton eventually brought the discourse to an end by snarling: "I've bloody 'ad enough of this," and plunged through the curtains a little like Eric Morecambe used to in his famous front-of-tabs sketches.

I gathered up my equipment and pulled back the curtain to find Zoe standing there, her eyes aglow. "Bloody hell," she said. "I wouldn't have missed that for anything."

If Hatton was everything I expected him to be, Jimmy Greaves certainly wasn't. Before we met, he was a man for whom I had nothing but the greatest respect. One of the few footballers on whom the label 'genius' could be stuck without fear of contradiction, he had also battled through the despair of alcoholism to re-invent himself as a television pundit. He was chirpy, witty and promised to be an ideal interviewee.

I met him at the *TV-am* studios in London, and it was clear from the start that he did not want to be there. He was not the least bit interested in anything I wanted to ask and resorted to grunts or monosyllabic replies. It all made for a pointless 15 minutes, and I still wonder why he agreed to the interview in the first place.

The shortest conversation I ever had with any celebrity was of my own making, and I don't regret a second of it. This unlikely confrontation happened in a Ryde car park one early summer evening. As I strode to my car at the end of the working day, I glanced across the car park and there in the far corner, the only other person in sight, was the unmistakable figure of Arthur Lowe. He had on one of those little peaked caps favoured by landlubbers who spend all their spare time playing on boats and he cut a faintly preposterous figure.

I had decided not to bother him, but something made me change my mind. As I strode across the car park towards him he seemed to shrivel in on himself in an effort to disappear. Here was a man who did not want to be bothered under any circumstances.

As soon as I arrived in front of him I said: "Good evening Mr Lowe. I have no intention of bothering you or even asking for an autograph. I would just like to shake your hand and thank you for all the pleasure you have given me over the years."

He glowered at me through those glasses, realised I meant it, and replied: "Well... I thank you so much. That's jolly kind of you." We shook hands and I walked away. A few months later he died in his dressing room while waiting to go on stage.

Whenever I am asked whether comedians are as funny offstage as on, the answer is usually no. Yet there was one star who was far funnier offstage than on, and he provided me with one of the most entertaining evenings I have ever spent.

Larry Grayson was appearing for a summer season at Sandown Pier on the Isle of Wight, and I was invited to his dressing room after the show to join the end-of-season party. It was not a prospect I anticipated with fervid excitement, but no excuse came readily to hand. The room was heaving with dancers and backstage staff. Grayson dispensed the gin and then sat there in a silk dressing gown while he regaled everyone with show-business anecdotes.

He was at his best while recalling the pitfalls of working in repertory and two of his stories have remained with me.

One involved a two-hour play, the denouement of which involved the leading lady snatching a gun from a drawer and shooting the leading man in the chest from point-blank range. The female lead was having an affair with the show's director and on this particular evening the two had a tiff just before the curtain went up, and the furious actress set about sabotaging the entire production.

No sooner had the curtain gone up, than she stormed across the stage, grabbed the gun and shot her bewildered co-star from no more than a foot away. He had no choice but to clutch his chest and fall to the floor 'dead.' This left the curtain operator with little option but to pull the tabs slowly together.

Grayson said he was waiting in the wings ready to go on, and he heard one elderly lady in the front row say to her friend: "Well, it wasn't bad. But it wasn't as long as I thought it would be."

It is clear that weapons presented something of an ever-present hazard to repertory actors, and Grayson went on to tell us about another play that relied for its thrilling climax on a servant girl snatching a shotgun from the wall and letting the dastardly lord of the manor have both barrels.

On this particular occasion the gun would not work. She pulled frantically at the triggers, banged the gun on the floor and squealed with frustration. But buckshot came there none. She did the only thing she could think of on the spur of the moment and walked up to the squire and kicked him squarely in the testicles.

To his eternal credit, he fell to the floor clutching his groin and shouting: "The boot was poisoned! The boot was poisoned!"

Towards the end of the evening I asked Grayson why he had never delivered any of this material on a talk show. He said, quite simply, that no-one had ever asked him.

The one man who would have provided Grayson with the perfect stage was Michael Parkinson, whose strength lies in the fact that he is happy to be the pedestal and not the statue. He allows people to display themselves and their talents uninhibited by the threat of their flow being interrupted by some smart remark. Over the course of more than 30 years he has made an art out of being an enthusiastic spectator, and while it may not have been fashionable at a time when coarseness is often confused with comedy and humiliation with entertainment, he has stayed the course by proving that there will always be a market for genuine family entertainment.

A few years ago Parkinson came down to take part in the Chichester Festivities and I was asked to interview him live in front of about 500 people in Chichester Cathedral. It promised to be a bit of an ordeal for both of us.

I was interviewing Britain's best-known interviewer, and he was placing his reputation in the hands of a provincial hack who had the ability (or lack of it) to drag him through the longest two hours of his life.

However, we hit it off almost as soon as we met, and I decided to do a Parky on him. I just sat back, pressed the right buttons and let him tell the anecdotes he was bound to have stored up over 30 years of interviewing everyone from Orson Welles to Billy Connolly; from John Wayne to Dame Sybil Thorndike. He quickly warmed to the task and the buttock-numbing seating arrangements in the cathedral were quickly forgotten as he evoked memories of Tommy Cooper, Eric Morecambe, Les Dawson and all the other comedians we took for granted until they were no longer there.

You could almost hear the bladders stretching as the audience did their best not to break the spell by traipsing off to the lavatory, and Parky offered them no relief by giving every sign of being able to go on for hours. It came to a reluctant conclusion on both sides, and as part of a foreword for a book a few months later he was kind enough to state that it had been one of the most enjoyable evenings he and his wife Mary had had for a long time. The feeling was mutual.

Another person whose company I enjoyed against all the odds was Russell Grant, then the fluffy astrologer on *TV-am*. At that time his syndicated astrology column was being published in well over 100 regional newspapers throughout the country and he impressed me by being able to name every publication and its editor on request.

He was also a man who believed in getting his money's worth wherever he went. Halfway through our chat at his home in Wembley he asked if I wanted some coffee. I followed him through to the kitchen which contained one of the largest refrigerators I had ever seen. He opened the door and there linings its shelves were hundreds of those little individual milk and cream containers you get in hotel rooms.

He noted my surprise and said: "Why not? I'm always staying in hotels and paying through the nose for the privilege. I've paid for 'em so I make sure I blooming well use 'em dear. Did you say cream or milk?"

CHAPTER FIVE

The days of Dylan, dinosaurs and the great unwashed

THE SIXTIES WAS the definitive era for the development of popular music in Britain and my generation has a sniffy regard for subsequent hybrids like glam rock, punk and the new romantics which were vapid spin-offs from a decade that saw our groups in glorious domination. I use the word 'group' deliberately, because in the sixties the word 'band' was invariably preceded by Salvation Army, brass or elastic.

As the sixties dawned, the Isle of Wight was not exactly in the throbbing forefront of all that was raw and innovative, despite the efforts of Ryde Borough Council. They had heard a vague rumour that something called The Beatles had recorded a little tune called *Ticket to Ride*, so in a moment of previously unsuspected inspiration they optimistically sent them four tickets to Ryde. Even now I find myself swooning at the sheer opportunism of it all. However, the town clerk had to inform the assembled burghers that 'the fabulous four' had decided not to avail themselves of their generous offer.

However, I do recall seeing The Rolling Stones performing in Ryde Pavilion a few months before they were brought to the attention of my parents' mortified generation. During their first appearance on *Top of the Pops*, I remember summoning my parents to the front-room, which they invariably evacuated at that time of the week. They regarded the first few bars of the theme music as the equivalent of an air-raid warning, and sought safe haven in the kitchen for half an hour.

However, as Mick Jagger strutted and flounced his way across the screen, his ears barely visible beneath floppy tresses, the chance to shock proved irresistible. "You have to see this bloke," I shouted and my mother and father peered round the door like missionaries at a freak show. You have to remember that only a little over 20 years earlier my father had been fighting his way back from the beaches of Dunkirk, and you just knew from looking at his face at that moment that he was seriously wondering whether it was worth the effort.

However, both my mother and father came to harbour a certain affection for the music of the decade and at the end of it they visited Afton Down for the largest of the Island's famous pop festivals. Almost as an after-thought they brought home a couple of hitch-hikers for a bath and something to eat before the grateful couple made their way back to the mainland.

For the first time since we imprisoned Charles I at Carisbrooke Castle and earned the undying appreciation of Cromwell and his surly followers, the pop festivals made the Isle of Wight seem historically significant. You knew something was happening that people would remember for years to come.

The first one was held in a barley field in Godshill in 1968 and was officially called The Great South Coast Bank Holiday Pop Festivity. The owner of the farm immediately came under enormous criticism for daring to make a few of his acres available for this extravaganza, and about a week before it was due to begin I was asked by the news desk of the Portsmouth *Evening News*, for whom I was then working as a district reporter, to contact this unfortunate man and do an update.

It was not my finest moment, and less than two minutes into the telephone conversation, he ordered me to bugger off. Remembering my father's maxim of 'treat everyone as you would wish to be treated, and failing that treat them as they treat you,' I suggested that he bugger off as well. It was not in the Noel Coward league of witty repartee, and the farmer felt so slighted he rang my editor, a formidable gentleman by the name of Howard Faircloth. Now Mr Faircloth (I still call him that to this day) had certain standards, and I was fairly certain they did not include swearing at interviewees. Only a month earlier he had told me to get my hair cut because I 'looked like a Teddy Boy,' so when the phone rang in the office and I heard his stern tones I could see my embryonic career coming to an unceremonious end.

The conversation went thus:

'Mr Newbery?'

'Yes Mr Faircloth.'

'I have just received a telephone call from a Mr Flux of Godshill who said you told him - and I quote - to bugger off. Is this true?'

'I'm afraid it is, yes.'

'May I ask why you tendered this particular piece of advice?'

'I was trying to do an update on the Island pop festival, he objected to the line of questioning and told me to bugger off. So I told him to do the same.'

'I see. In your position I would probably have done the same, but kindly do not make a habit of it. Good day.'

That's one of the reasons I am still delighted to meet up with the old fellow for lunch more than 30 years on. He taught me a lesson I have always tried to carry into my editorships over the years - respect the people who work for you, and suspect the people you work for. Unfortunately, far too many people take the easy option and do it the other way round with disastrous consequences.

The Godshill festival was originally conceived as a fund-raising event in aid of the village swimming pool (they still haven't got one more than 30 years later) by brothers Ray and Ron Foulk. It is strange to think that if they had opted for a jumble sale or a whist drive, three of the most exotic years in the history of the Isle of Wight might never have happened.

Distance has lent a little romanticism to the Godshill festival, but it had the ramshackle air of an event that had been arranged by people more used to staging jumble sales. It lasted one night, but it did manage to attract some well-known acts of the day including The Move, Jefferson Airplane, the Crazy World of Arthur Brown, Fairport Convention, the Pretty Things and a curly-haired little chap called Marc Bolan who, with his mate, then luxuriated in the name of Tyrannosaurus Rex. They were way down the bill.

Arthur Brown had intended to turn up by hot-air balloon, but the gusty weather put paid to that. It also dealt a fatal blow to his stage act, which comprised entirely of his setting light to his head while singing his only hit, 'Fire.'

About 10,000 people attempted to make themselves comfortable on barley stubble, the weather was inhospitable for the time of year, the stage comprised four lorry trailers parked next to each other, food and drink were available at extortionate prices and toilet facilities consisted of a vast trench into which, in the early hours of the morning, one man was reported to have fallen head first.

We were never able to substantiate the story, but it did give rise to my favourite Isle of Wight limerick:

There was a young man from Ryde
Who fell into a cesspit and died.
He had a young brother
Who fell in another
And now they're in turd side by side.

Everyone who attended Godshill took away their own memories, but my favourite is attributed to Iain Matthews of Fairport Convention. He said: "We used to play a very long version of Leonard Cohen's *Suzanne*. I remember closing my eyes at the beginning of the song, and when I opened them at the end, dawn had broken. In one song it had gone from pitch dark to morning. It freaked the shit out of me."

The festival was greeted by the Isle of Wight establishment in much the same way that Queen Victoria would have greeted a streaker - with a mixture of fear, outrage and mild curiosity. Council chambers rang with the indignation of double-barrelled members who feared for everything from the wellbeing of the Island's reputation as a centre for family holidays, to the contamination of the ferries bringing the great unwashed from all corners of Britain.

"Never will we allow such a catastrophe to befall the Island again!" they bellowed.

The following year's festival was bigger, better and benefited directly from the publicity generated by its little brother 12 months earlier. All that umbrage, which had hissed and snorted its way out of the Island had a profound effect on the stars of the day and the people who had made them what they were. This was the dawning of the age of free love, free speech, and the freedom to do what you wanted, with whoever you wanted, wherever you wanted. If this sort of behaviour caused vexation to your parents and their peers, then that just added to the fun. All of a sudden the Island became a focal point for the young to flaunt their new-found liberation. If stuffy, old establishment figures got themselves worked up over a little overnight shindig like Godshill, what would they do if a real festival landed in their midst?

The Foulk Brothers were determined to find out. They had now joined forces with a promoter called Rikki Farr, and Fiery Creations was formed. Farr, the son of former heavyweight boxing champion Tommy Farr, was a self-publicist of the type much coveted by reporters, because he tended to do our job for us. We stood there with pencils poised over notebooks, and Farr filled in the blanks. We became accustomed to his outrageous plans, but there was one extraordinary rumour that would not go away.

Bob Dylan, folk music guru, protest singer, one of the most original talents ever to emerge from the United States - and a reclusive figure for the past three years since he almost lost his life in a motorcycle accident - was rumoured to be making his live comeback on the Isle of Wight. Yes Rikki. Of course Rikki. Anything you say Rikki.

To put this unlikely event into some perspective, it was as if Marlon Brando had signed up for a season of repertory at the Pavilion Theatre in Ryde, or that Henry Kissinger was in the running for the job of town clerk with Newport Borough Council.

Bob Dylan and the Isle of Wight? The Isle of Wight and Bob Dylan? No matter how you rearranged the words, the very idea was preposterous. It met with impressive amounts of derision, especially from the hacks on the music papers in London. Response on the Island was mixed. The older generation reckoned that as he was American he must be some relation to Marshall Dillon, shops ran out of Vaseline as the more aware businessmen never stopped licking their lips for six months, and the kids thought that anyone who could attract The Beatles to the Island was all right by them. The most poignant reaction came from members of the Isle of Wight Folk Club, who used to meet in the early sixties at The Sloop Inn in Wootton. As one of them said to me at the time: "If it's true, it's like the second coming. But we simply cannot believe that Bob Dylan will be appearing in a field less than a mile from our pub as the pig flies."

But the Foulks and Farr had actually pulled it off, and on the evening of August 31, 1969, an estimated 100,000 people gathered in a Wootton meadow to watch the great man perform for less than an hour. Among those in the VIP enclosure were three of the Beatles (McCartney never turned up), Jane Fonda, Keith Richard and many stars of the moment who would barely turn a head these days if they were to walk naked down Pall Mall, like Peter Wyngarde and Francoise Hardy.

The stories surrounding Dylan's imminent arrival were as nothing compared to those that circulated after he had left. He stayed for a week at Forelands Farm, Bembridge, with George Harrison as his house guest and there was talk of a jamming session at one of the local hostelries, the Crab and Lobster. It later transpired that this was just one of the rumours that had been put about by amused locals who had discovered that they newspaper fellers from the mainland would believe anything you told them about the Isle of Wight, and some would even pay for such information.

One anecdote that was true, however, concerned a game of doubles that took place on the tennis court at Forelands Farm. It featured Dylan and John Lennon against Ringo Starr and George Harrison, and it was Harrison's wife at the time, Patti Boyd, who pointed out that there could hardly have been two more exclusive pairings in the history of the game.

There was an unexpected reaction to the festival. Against all the odds, the majority of people seemed to have liked it. Even the local newspapers, which were scarcely regarded as the natural mouthpieces of the young, expressed grudging approval. My own, the *Portsmouth Evening News* as it was then called, came over all new age in its leader column, purring: "A large part of a glacier of prejudice melted away this weekend. Let the hippies ring out their little bells, for social history was made in that Island field." I knew all the leader writers at the time (many of whom still had their own teeth) and I still can't believe that one of them came out with that.

The *IW County Press*, perhaps disappointed at the lack of mayhem and the shortage of people taking uncivil liberties, felt the event was 'more like a Hindu prayer meeting on the Ganges than a music festival in our garden isle.' It was a perplexing observation and one, I suspect, made from a safe distance.

The consequences of Mr Dylan's Island sojourn were far longer, louder and more dramatic than he had been. When it became clear that the organisers had now acquired a taste for festivals, there was a sudden flurry of public meetings, residents associations were formed throughout the East Wight and the Isle of Wight County Council began much loud harrumphing. So many of its members seemed to be retired servicemen, that reports of meetings sounded like communiques from a war council - which, in effect, they were. The battle was on to prevent another festival, and leading it was Alderman Mark Woodnutt, who also happened to be the Island's MP.

He began urgent attempts to get legislation through parliament that would give local authorities the power to refuse permission 'for more than 50 people to sleep overnight in a temporary encampment.' It was a 'ban the pop festival' bill in all but name, and Woodnutt came out with increasingly extravagant pronouncements to back his campaign to be seen as the white knight who was galloping to rescue a beleaguered population from the scourge of drugs, long hair, silly clothes and the tendency to piddle under a hedge when a trip to the nearest latrine and back meant missing Tom Paxton's entire set.

On one occasion, Woodnutt said: "I am not a prude and I do not mind nude bathing at the right place at the right time. But I do not like fornicating on the beach, which is what we have been seeing." It came as an immense relief to Islanders that their MP did not like fornicating on the beach.

On another occasion, he proclaimed: "The organisers of last year's festival are planning a similar event next year, and if the local authority is not, by then, in possession of powers to lay down and enforce sanitation regulations, the health of everyone on the Island will be endangered. It needs only a hot, dry weekend to bring about an epidemic."

It sounded ludicrous at the time and sounds even more so now. The 1970 festival at Afton Down in Freshwater was staged over five gloriously hot days, and I witnessed there the ultimate in questionable sanitation and hygiene. The toilets were plywood cubicles with no doors and the 'drainage' consisted of a trench. A little man-made hillock had at the top a bouquet of taps pointing in all directions. Under each was a trough, down which the water gushed day and night. It was used for everything, but, unfortunately, usually not in the right order. The people at the top of the hill would be rinsing their underwear under the taps, and the water was then flowing down to the people below who were filling their kettles with it.

Yet the Island was not struck down by dysentery or malaria, and the only people left feeling really sick were the Foulk brothers and Rikki Farr. They had pressed ahead with plans for their 1970 extravaganza, and the list of performers ensured that it would be remembered as one of the finest festivals the world had ever seen. *The Melody Maker* described it as 'the five days that shook the world.' That may have been overstating it a little, but when an estimated 500,000 people descended upon the Island for the third - and what turned out to be the last - festival, the old place certainly shuddered a bit.

Among those appearing were The Who, The Doors, Joan Baez, Joni Mitchell, Emerson, Lake and Palmer, Jethro Tull, Leonard Cohen, Miles Davis and (a surprise hit with his rendering of *There'll Always be an England*) Tiny Tim. But the star attraction was Jimi Hendrix, who was eventually slain by his drugs addiction less than three weeks after performing there.

But far from being a festival of love (you will recall we were enjoined to make plenty of that in those days, but preferably not on the beach lest Mr Woodnutt be watching) the 1970 festival was riven by disputes between the organisers and the stars. Then raw commerce raised its ugly head. Attracting the cream of the world's artists to a field on the west coast of the Isle of Wight did not come cheap, so tickets had to reflect the outlay. They were expensive for the time, so a bunch of troublemakers made it their business to pull down the perimeter fences in an attempt to get in for nothing. Eventually the organisers had no option but to bow to mob rule, and tens of thousands gained free access. This was in addition to the thousands who simply perched on the surrounding downland for the entire five days and watched for nothing anyway.

It's hardly surprising, then, that Mark Woodnutt's successful campaign to obtain local authority control for such events was all in vain. He was pushing against an open door by this time, because Fiery Creations had had enough. One of the Foulk brothers told a Press conference: "There won't be anymore festivals. What started as a beautiful dream just got out of hand. We've had enough."

And what of Woodnutt's dire predictons? Well, the Island's chief medical officer said he was satisfied with general standards of hygiene during the festival, and the litter left afterwards did not constitute a health hazard. Hampshire's chief constable, Douglas Osmond, put on his civvies and sat among the crowd, afterwards observing that 'there was less violence there than at a normal league football match.'

And what of Mr Woodnutt himself? Well, he remained the Island's MP for another four years. During that time the BBC exposed his part in a land scam, and the electorate booted him out of office at the first opportunity in 1974.

The three pop festivals have now become part of Island folklore, and I was privileged to play a small part in the massive coverage they received throughout the world. As a young Islander more than 30 years ago, I supported them fully and was grateful for the credibility they gave to the place of my birth.

As a middle-aged Islander at the start of the 21st century, I still believe the festival legacy has done the place far more good than harm. And if the interest my children have shown in the events is anything to go by, it will live on.

CHAPTER SIX

Vicars, bodies and a visit to Britt Ekland

AT A TIME when you can send a message to the other side of the world at the press of a button, contact almost everyone by telephone and watch bemused while kids text their friends rather than walk next door to engage them in conversation, the importance newspapers placed on personal contact back in the sixties now seems rather quaint.

Every Tuesday morning on the *Isle of Wight Times*, I would embark upon my vicar run. This meant pottering around the parishes of Ryde in my little red Mini calling on as many clergymen as possible. They fell into two distinct categories. Those who made a point of being in at roughly the same time every week and seemed genuinely pleased to divest themselves of information about deaths, harvest festivals and the local Mothers' Union, and those who made a point of never being in no matter what time of the day, week - or even year - I called.

The warmest welcome came primarily from the representatives of the Church of England, while the non-conformists were mostly unavailable. There was one who was always rather sweaty, breathless and dishevelled every time he answered the door, and gave the impression of having been disturbed at an inopportune moment. The depths of his home had a discouraging mustiness about it and he also had an unnerving habit of calling me 'young boy,' while rubbing his hands together in what I took to be some sort of misplaced anticipation. After two visits he was inked heavily in the address book as 'phone only.'

The Anglican priests existed mostly in shabby grandeur, rattling around in huge vicarages with a wife, a few kids and not much money to keep them going. This was just before the advent of trendy vicars who, in the seventies, emerged from theological colleges with hairstyles like Keith Moon, wives who looked like Joni Mitchell and a tendency to say 'hi' rather than 'hello.' None of my Protestants came into that category. They were of the pre-war vintage, amiable but strictly conventional, and when you met for a chat in their study their wives would suddenly waft in unbidden with a tray containing cups, saucers, a pot of tea, a little milk jug and a bowl of sugar lumps complete with tiny tongs.

The vicar would then do the honours while enquiring after your wellbeing and career prospects. In the background Brahms would be murmuring from an old gramophone, the autumn sun would be slanting in through dusty windows and you would tuck into a few Nice biscuits while the conversation meandered slowly all over the place. They used phrases like 'the unfortunate deceased' and 'the little ones in my flock' without ever sounding pompous or preposterous, and talking to them was like slowly slipping into a warm bath - comfortable and reassuring.

These occasions had nothing to do with news or journalism and everything to do with getting to know your patch and making contacts you hoped would one day pay off by way of an innocent tip-off that would lead to a story of national significance. They never did of course, but I look back on those times with immense affection. One vicar, the Rev James Buckett of St Helens, impressed me so much with his warmth, friendliness and unfailing good nature that 15 years after we first met (by which time he had become Canon Buckett of St Thomas' Church in Newport) I asked him if he would christen my daughter Samantha. As he applied the sign of the cross to her forehead I remember thinking that it meant much more than it might otherwise have done because it had been carried out by a man of such obvious goodness.

Undertakers were another invaluable source of information for a trainee reporter, and one of them in particular was an indefatigably cheerful man who never let business interfere with pleasure. I would often see him at a local hostelry, outside of which he would park his magnificent hearse complete with occupied coffin.

"If anyone asks," he would say, "I tell them I'm on my way to meet a client. If the client is already on board it doesn't really matter because I've never had one complain yet about being kept waiting while I have a pint." When you spend your life surrounded by grief, formaldehyde, piped organ music and the vile stench of lilies, such an attitude must be essential. It is not a job I could ever do, though on one occasion the opportunity to carry out a little work experience came a little too close for comfort.

When someone especially well-known within the community dies, the bereaved are deemed worthy of a personal visit from a representative of the local newspaper. It is not the sort of meeting either party anticipates with much relish to begin with, and people always assume that the last thing grieving relatives want is to be bothered by the Press. But more often than not they are flattered by the attention being paid to their loved one, and clergymen often acted as intermediaries to help me gain access because they felt it assisted the mourning process. It meant sitting there for up to two hours at a time chronicling some fairly mediocre achievements and helping the family plough through a boxful of photograph albums.

The predominant memories I have of making what is rather luridly known in journalism as 'the death knock' is the amount of Battenburg cake I consumed. For some reason, Battenburg is the preferred confection of the bereaved, and to this day I cannot munch on a slice without being whisked back 40 years to a succession of tiny, darkened frontrooms and murmured conversations conducted against the background of muffled sobs.

However, while I accepted that meeting the bereaved was part of my job as a junior hack, I drew the line at direct association with the dead. The ultimate confrontation almost occurred, however, when I visited the home of a leading Spiritualist who had 'passed over' only 24 hours before. I was met at the front door by a woman dressed from head to toe in black, and with her face covered by a dark veil. She stared at me for a disconcertingly long period of time before speaking.

"We were told you would be coming," she said in an ancient, croaky voice laden with foreboding. As she led me into what can only be described as a parlour, where candles threw spooky shadows, photographs were draped in dark cloth and ancient sofas were covered with antimacassars, I began to wonder what dark arts had been employed to foretell my arrival. Had the news been divulged in a séance? Had a long-dead relative popped back with the information. Had a Red Indian spirit guide (they all have Red Indian spirit guides) been the messenger.

"Actually," she replied. "The vicar rang."

It was not the most auspicious start to an interview, but it was not long before the photo albums came out and I began to scribble down the usual details about war service, work record and devotion to the Spiritualist church. It was just when the Battenburg cake had arrived and the conversation had begun to settle into a familiar rhythm that the first heart-breaking wail rent the air.

"Oooooooohh Cyril, please do wake up. Oh darling, please." Listening to the sound of somebody's heart breaking is not to be recommended, but this even had special effects added. As that first shriek ricocheted despairingly around the silent house, lightning flashed and thunder rumbled. It was like being trapped on the set of a cheap Hammer horror.

The old woman continued thumbing through the album as though nothing had happened and I sat there wondering whether I had imagined the whole weird moment. I was about to check a date or something equally incongruous, when the anguish from the bedroom above began again.

"Ooooooh please darling, please, please, PLEASE! You must wake up. I can't bear it. I simply can't bear it when you act like this!"

Suddenly there was a loud bump, and I could control myself no longer. "Christ," I blurted out, "it sounds as though she really has woken him up."

The old woman rose slowly from her chair, raised a hand to me as though stopping traffic, and began to make her way laboriously up the stairs. There followed a mumbled conversation punctuated by forlorn cries and 'ssshhhing' noises. Footsteps then began to descend the stairs as the thunder growled in the distance. By now I was in such a state that I had seriously begun to wonder which of the three would be coming through the door.

To my relief it was the old woman. "Young man," she said, "you will have gathered that my sister does not believe that her husband has passed over. She thinks he is sleeping and in her efforts to awaken him she has pulled his body off the bed. I have two favours to ask of you. Firstly, would you be kind enough to help me put him back...?"

I have no idea what the second favour was. By the time she had asked it, I was out of the house, up the path and roaring down the road in my Mini.

However, I managed to get off lightly compared to the *County Press* reporter who, legend has it, was prevailed upon to call at the Bembridge home of a recently-dead admiral back in the 1920s. It was the twilight of a winter's day when he eventually found the place and cycled up the long, gravel path towards the Gothic pile in the distance. As he pounded on the front door, the sound seemed to reverberate throughout the entire building. Just as he had given up hope of finding anyone home, he heard the sound of a latch being lifted and the huge oak door was slowly pulled open far enough for a face to peer round.

It belonged to an old woman. "Well?" she said querulously.

The reporter swallowed hard. "I'm awfully sorry to bother you at such an inopportune moment," he said, "but I'm from the *County Press*. We have heard the sad news of the admiral's passing and we wish to pay a fulsome tribute to his quite extraordinary life. I wondered, therefore, whether it would be possible to get some appropriate details."

"I haven't much time to waste on such things," said the woman, "so ask your questions quickly if you please and be gone."

"Well," said the reporter, turning up the collar of his overcoat as the wind began to whoop and whine around the gables of the old house, "could I begin by asking what year he joined the Royal Navy?"

The old woman closed her eyes and began to search her memory. "I believe it was in 18... no, that's the year we were married. It must have been in... no, no his father was still alive then." Suddenly her eyes opened and they glistened with inspiration. "I know how I can find out. Come with me."

The door creaked open a few feet further and the reporter squeezed through to find himself in a huge hall, festooned with cobwebs upon which newer cobwebs had been spun. It was gloomy, grubby and the odour of neglect was everywhere.

"Well come along then," snapped the old woman as she began to shuffle down a long passageway, to which there seemed no end, just a deepening darkness. The reporter quickly followed and the woman turned into the kitchen. There, on the table, lay the naked corpse of her husband.

She picked up his left arm and, starting at his wrist, began to work her way up his tattoos. “Ah, I knew it was here somewhere,” she trilled triumphantly, jabbing at a pale blue number etched on the old boy’s bicep. “It was 1852!”

People whose work constantly brings them into contact with death inevitably become rather blasé about it and practical jokes are used to help break up the grim monotony. One of the most wicked I ever heard about involved members of a local constabulary on the mainland. Whenever a rookie constable joined the team, they would take him down to the mortuary and pretend to involve him in the jape.

“This is a laugh,” they would say. “If you climb on to one of the tables, we will cover you with a sheet and you pretend to be dead. Then we will bring in a young policewoman who has just joined us and has to get used to viewing bodies. When we pull your sheet back, you can suddenly sit upright and she’ll be bloody terrified.”

Flattered to be included in the joke, the young policeman would do as he was told and lay on the table with other bodies all around him. His ‘mates’ would switch off the light and shut the door as they left because ‘it’s got to look right when we come back.’

The young policeman would then be left on his own in the silent, darkened mortuary for about five minutes while his imagination began to produce its own demons. Suddenly, the ‘body’ to his right would reach across, gently touch his arm and say: “Bloody cold in here isn’t it?”

One policeman is said to have screamed so loud that he lost his voice for three days, while another was shaking so much when his laughing colleagues returned that he jabbed himself in the eye while attempting to replace his spectacles and was off sick for three weeks.

I eventually developed a network of people in the towns and villages surrounding Ryde, on whom I called for pleasure as much as information. One of them was Gerald Caws who owned a shoe shop in Seaview. He must hold the record for the person whose name I typed the most number of times in my career, because he was an exceptional gardener and seemed to win virtually every class he entered in every horticultural show we covered. I once suggested to Clive Barton that it would save time if, instead of printing the full results, we simply stated: “These are the classes not won by Gerald Caws.” But Barton had a paper to fill, and if that had to be accomplished by printing the same name about 80 times, then so be it.

Like most of my contacts, however, though Gerald knew what was going on in his community, he did not really have any idea what constituted a news story. There was no shame in this, as I was equally ignorant about what comprised a classic suede brogue, but as if to prove the point, a national story happened literally in his backyard and I found out about it purely by accident.

I was sitting in his shop one morning enjoying a cup of coffee, when one of his staff came in from the back and announced: "I've thrown the stuffed elephant down there now and it's still not full." Gerald, never a man to get over-excited about anything, simply shrugged and continued telling me about a well-known stalwart of the village football club committee who had just died.

"Sorry to interrupt Gerald," I said, "but that lady has just thrown a what down where?"

"Oh that," he replied. "A damned great hole suddenly appeared out the back first thing this morning and we have been throwing all our rubbish down there as we try to fill it up. Handy really."

We wandered out the back and there indeed was a damned great hole at the bottom of which, and barely discernible, was a huge, pink, stuffed elephant. The vast chasm turned out to be some ancient well that nobody knew existed, and Gerald was more than delighted to see his shop featured in the national newspapers a couple of days later.

News sense is an unimportant but elusive quality. You either possess it or you don't. It is an instinct, and therefore difficult to teach. The phrase 'that's a good story' springs instantly into the minds of those who are born with a news sense, and would never occur to those who aren't. There is a well-known story - I have no idea whether or not it is apocryphal - about a report sent to a local newspaper from a Mothers' Union meeting. It began with all the usual information about the president welcoming new members, approving the minutes of the previous meeting, introducing the speaker, announcing the winner of the raffle etc.

It ended with the words: "Unfortunately, Miss Jones was unable to complete her cookery demonstration. To the consternation of those in attendance, her flambe caught the hall curtains alight and by the time the fire brigade arrived the building had been burned to the ground. Next month's meeting will be held at the Sunday School."

Another regular port of call for trainee journalists are at homes where an elderly couple are celebrating their golden or even diamond wedding anniversary. It's usually a straightforward job. The old folk are photographed either in a gentle hug on the settee, eyes glowing with long-lasting love, or brandishing champagne glasses with pictures of the family arranged all around. They then tell the reporter that the secret of a long and happy marriage is give and take, they josh each other about memories of their first date at which point the teapot is produced and everyone sits down to a cuppa and a slice of commemorative cake.

On one particular occasion, however, things failed to run their normal course. I was just leaving the *IW Times*' office one winter's evening when the phone rang. A man told me that his neighbours were celebrating their diamond wedding anniversary the next day, and he wondered whether we would be interested in putting an article in the paper. I took a note of the name and address and turned up unexpectedly the next morning.

The house was unmistakable, especially in the confines of the dainty cul-de-sac. All around were neat little bungalows, and right in the middle of them was one that looked as though Armagh prison had crept there one night and pupped. The paintwork was brown (by design rather than deterioration), every window was covered by a panel of chicken wire, the grass in the front garden was about two feet high and chained to a flimsy-looking post was a dog that looked like a cross between a rottweiller and a kimodo dragon. It growled at me, its red eyes glowing and its tongue flickering as though enjoying the taste of my fear.

Suddenly the front door was flung open and standing there was the fattest man I had ever seen. His stomach descended in primeval ledges down his body until the subsidence finally halted around his knees. A string vest struggled to contain the bulk, and braces struggled to contain the string vest.

But it was his head that was the most transfixing. Completely shaven, it looked as though it had been subjected to immense pressure from both sides so that his eyes were so close together that he appeared almost Cyclopean, his nose was preposterously aquiline and his mouth had been squashed into a circle, so that he looked permanently surprised or on the point of whistling. The next time I saw anything remotely like this, it was wearing an apron and starring in the *Texas Chain Saw Massacre*.

We looked at each other, me unable to speak and he apparently incapable of doing so. Eventually he said: "Wot?" It sounded rude, but I suspect it was the longest sentence he was capable of uttering. I found myself replying more slowly than usual.

"Good morning. I understand Mr and Mrs Jenkins (not their real names) who I believe live at this address are celebrating their diamond wedding today. I'm from the local newspaper and I was wondering if they would care to talk to me about it."

It was difficult to decide whether he hadn't heard or hadn't understood. Either way, his face did not register the slightest cognitive flicker. I decided to try again. "Sorry to bother...?"

"Muuhhh!" he bellowed. It was a bovine noise that had the desired effect. A minute later his mother squeezed her head beneath his left arm and rested it on the side of his chest. So vast was he and so small was she that she looked like a cameo brooch.

"Congratulations," I said, "on your 60th wedding anniversary."

"Ooo told you?"

"One of your neighbours was kind enough..."

"You bastards!" she shrieked at the street in general.

"Basserds!" bellowed her first born.

"I'm sorry if..."

"Not your fault," she said. "It is me anniversary today, but the bastards down this road knows bloody well I haven't spoke to my old man for nigh on 20 years."

"I'm sorry. We got a call last evening to say that you both lived here."

"We do."

"You mean you both live in this house, you've been married for 60 years and you haven't spoken to each other for 20 of them?"

"S'right."

My news sense, such as it as at that time, evaporated. There was a national story right in front of me - couple married for 60 years and haven't spoken to each other for 20 of them despite sharing the same home. I should have grasped the situation, taken the interview by the scruff of the neck and started to collect the facts. What I actually said was: "Do you...? Have the...? Did they...? What will...?"

Cyclops sensed my discomfort and decided to add to it. "'S'off!" he bellowed. His mother, to whom I was beginning to warm, twanged his left braces strap against his nipple and Cyclops squealed.

"Don't you mind 'im my cocker," she said. "Daft great bugger 'e is. Would you like a cuppa tea then?"

"No thanks," I replied, and Cyclops slunk back towards the house, standing in the doorway to give me one last baleful glare. "But I would like to know why you and your husband have bothered to stay together all this time."

"It was 'is fault," she said, pointing towards her son. "Me and the old man fought over his custody. Neither of us wanted the bugger, so we both ended up with 'im. Fer life by the look of it."

She trudged back into the house, thumping her son on the shoulder to get him to move out of her way, the way a herdsman would a lazy bullock. I made my way back to the car, and a chap across the road looked up from clipping his hedge and smirked.

A journalist without a news sense has little future in the profession and will soon be found out. But that doesn't mean we can always find a story, even when we know it has happened. I recall, to my shame, being involved in the hunt for one major disaster that had happened just off the coast of the Isle of Wight, and not being able to find it.

It was a Friday night and I was at home watching a horror film with my then fiancee Denise, when a news flash suddenly appeared at the foot of the

screen. 'Oil tanker reported ablaze south-west of Isle of Wight. More soon."
I realised immediately that as duty reporter, my weekend was about to be cancelled.

Sure enough, the phone rang about two minutes later. It was the news editor at Portsmouth, Bernard King. "I take it you've heard? Nip over there, see what's going on and let me know. Thanks."

The south-west coast has always been my favourite part of the Island, and it has a certain charm even in the early hours of the morning. As we made our way from Ventnor along the Undercliff, there were little knots of people gathered at vantage points and peering out to sea. We stopped to join them.

"Seen anything?"

"Nah. I reckon somebody's having a laugh. If there really was a tanker on fire out there, you would see the glow in the sky if nothing else."

It seemed a reasonable point, but we moved on until we reached the Buddle Inn at Niton, where about 20 people were gazing out to sea.

"Seen anything?"

"Nah. I've just come down from Blackgang (a few miles further up the coast) and there's not a bloody thing. I'm off home."

Amid much disgruntled muttering, people padded off towards their cars, deeply disappointed at not being able to witness a tragedy unfold before their very eyes. We got back home and I phoned Bernard with the fateful words: "Nothing in it mate. It must have gone out."

About three weeks later, the tanker was still ablaze off the Island. And about three years later colleagues were still reminding me of the cock-up.

George Godden was not with me on that occasion. Had he been, and had we actually spotted the burning hulk, he would no doubt have attempted to get me as close as possible to it in a rowing boat, with the intention of producing a photograph that had the caption: 'Drama at sea as a brave rescuer attempts to approach the inferno.'

It is a good photographer's task to obtain a unique perspective of whatever job he or she attends - and George was a good photographer. One of the first assignments we undertook together was an oil slick that had appeared at Freshwater. As we drove over, George was already anticipating the shot. "Bound to be some birds or something covered in oil. This one won't take a minute."

We arrived at Freshwater beach and, thank goodness, there was no black, floundering wildlife to be seen. However, the oil was clearly visible on the pebbles. George sniffed deeply and wandered back to the seawall and back down to the beach again. But the only available wildlife was the wary looking reporter to his right.

"Tell you what Keef. If you get a bit closer to the surf, we'll do one of those 'a local man looks on sadly as the oil slick reaches the shore' sort of pictures.

There is only one thing a young reporter enjoys more than seeing his name in the paper, and that's seeing his face. I leapt into focus, looking as regretful as I could.

"Bit closer mate. Bit closer. Great. Great. Bit closer. Now look down at the oil."

I couldn't really miss it. It was lapping all over my shoes and my unhappiness was apparent. It was compounded the following day when a picture of me - from the ankles down - appeared in the newspaper with the caption: 'Police and coastguards are warning the public not to get too near to the oil that has washed up on Freshwater beach.'

Press photographers are as cynical as they come, but most are capable of turning into pussycats when in the presence of a famous woman who features high on their list of fantasy creatures. Back in the eighties, Fern Britton, now the popular co-presenter of *Good Morning*, was a Meridian presenter in Southampton and the opportunity arose for me to interview her when I was working for *The News* in Portsmouth.

Spotting the job on the diary, photographer Bill Shimmin immediately volunteered himself for it. We met Fern in some sort of play area near the studios, and Bill happily clicked away as she - in a pair of skintight jeans - posed on the swings and the roundabout. It was only when Shimmin's eye was red-raw and weeping from staring through his viewfinder at the object of his desire that we were able to settle down for a chat.

Those who have seen Fern on television and think she is a lovely, friendly, sexy lady are wrong. She is actually far nicer than that in every way and poor old Bill was visibly melting in her presence. I had begun to ask her a question about an area of her life - I forget what it was now - that she obviously found a bit boring and she replied: "Whenever people ask me that, I usually say, yeah, yeah, yeah, and I give a good blow-job as well."

Shimmin dropped his expensive camera. And it remains the only time I have ever heard a grown man whimper.

Another photographer at Portsmouth with very firm ideas about his choice in women was Roland Glass. He was devoted to (among others) Britt Ekland, and when the opportunity came for me to interview her in London in the eighties, he was the first among several volunteers. We turned up at her hotel suite, and one of the most beautiful women I have ever seen opened the door. It was her assistant, and she led us into the sitting room. By this time, Glass was trailing behind me like a cocker spaniel, eyes twinkling and tongue lolling.

We were invited to sit on a couple of tall, high-backed chairs and informed that 'Miss Ekland vill be viz you in a moment.' Roland, not exactly a giant among men, hauled himself up on to one of the chairs and his feet, quite literally, didn't touch the ground.

When Britt Ekland swept in he sat there with his head on one side staring in enraptured silence. She was exquisite in every way, charming, obliging, chatty and glorious to look at. After about ten minutes, I suggested we get some pictures done at which point Roland coughed. Britt squealed and jumped, and I can only presume she either had not noticed him or thought I was an amateur ventriloquist and had brought my dummy along for company.

They were the worst pictures Roland ever took. His finger was shaking so much that he kept missing his button. This was no hardship as far as I was concerned, since Britt had decided that a good picture would be one of her cuddling me. We remained in each other's arms while Roland juddered and swayed his way to the end of the job. I still cannot hear the Alison Moyet song *I Go Weak in the Presence of Beauty* without conjuring up a mental image of one little photographer and a Nikon that, on that day at least, had a life of its own.

The most naturally-talented photographer I ever worked with was Murray Sanders, who joined the *Weekly Post* as a 17-year-old back in the seventies and is now one of the top snappers on the *Daily Mail*. There was nothing I could teach Murray about photography for two very sound reasons - I didn't know anything about it myself and the gift he had was heaven-sent. I did know what I wanted in a picture for a local newspaper however, and it was not art. It was at this stage in his professional development that Murray and I occasionally fell out.

I once sent him to take a photograph of a girl who was one of the finest swimmers on the Island and was being tipped for national honours. He came back with one that he had taken of her as she executed a tumble turn at the end of a pool. Featuring prominently were the right hand side of her distorted mouth as she gasped for breath, most of her right armpit and lots of bubbles. He proudly placed it on the desk in front of me.

"What the hell's that?"

"It's that swimming girl."

"It's an armpit."

"Yeah, but it's her armpit."

"So your mum's got pictures of your armpits on her sideboard has she?"

"No, but it's an action shot."

"It's a bloody armpit."

"So you want me to get a picture of her face then?"

"That would be nice."

"I thought I was being artistic."

"You were. But I don't want art, I want faces. That's what sells me newspapers. You can do art when you get on the nationals. Until then it's faces."

Murray is now doing both with great aplomb and high levels of skill on the *Mail*, and though his photographs afforded me great pleasure as his career developed, it was his weakness as an animal lover that provided one of my favourite memories. One stiflingly hot August day, Murray and reporter Richard Wright were driving through the village of Newchurch in Murray's Mini. He slowed down when he saw a huge sheepdog standing on the pavement. "That dog," announced Murray with the instinct that some people have for these sort of things, "is lost."

Richard dismissed this shaft of perception and they went about their business. Half an hour later, on the way back, there was the same dog in the same place on the same pavement. Vindicated and slightly annoyed that his concerns had been ignored earlier, Murray stopped the car and rummaged around in the dog's fur for its collar. There on the name-tag was its name and an address in Cowes, about 12 miles away.

"There you are!" said Murray. "We're going to take him home." So a six-foot six-inch photographer, a six-foot reporter and a colossal sheepdog made their way in a Mini across the Isle of Wight on one of the hottest days of the year. They drove around Cowes for 15 minutes until they found the address. The little sliding windows on the Mini did not provide sufficient oxygen, and by now both men stank of sweat and dog. The condensation was running down the inside of the Mini in torrents.

Murray dragged the dog up the path and knocked on the door. A man answered. "Yeah?"

"I've brought your dog back," said our proud photographer.

"Nothing to do with me mate," said the man. "The bloke that owns him moved to Newchurch three days ago."

The strangest photographer I ever worked with was Adam Jones (not his real name for reasons that will become apparent). He seemed to appear out of nowhere looking for a job. He was a quietly-spoken man who liked a drink and would often talk about his time as a parachutist, a hovercraft pilot or as a member of Her Majesty's special services who did a lot but were not allowed to talk about it. I had him marked down as a fantasist, but he was a likable man who turned in some good photographs.

One Boxing Day morning I had a call from the police.

"Mr Newbery?"

"Speaking."

"Ryde police station here sir. We have a man in custody who says he works for you. His name is Adam Jones."

"That's right. He's our photographer. Why, what's the problem."

"Well sir, yesterday we had reason to arrest Mr Jones for taking a vehicle without permission."

"Oh no. Whose car was it?"

"It wasn't a car sir. It was a hovercraft..."

Apparently Adam had been alone and drunk on Christmas Day and wandered down to Ryde seafront. There on the foreshore were a couple of hovercraft used to service what was then the world's only passenger hovercraft service. He simply got in one, started it up and headed out into the Solent. The thing about hovercraft is that they make a hell of a noise and it wasn't long before the whole of Ryde Esplanade was peering out from behind its curtains to herald the advent of a previously-unsuspected Christmas Day service.

A company pilot was summoned and there then followed the strangest police chase the Island has ever seen, with hovercraft in pursuit of hovercraft up and down Spithead. The company pilot said that in his view the craft being piloted by Adam was never in any sort of trouble or difficulty and he only brought the escapade to an end when he got bored.

The resultant case attracted Fleet Street's finest and on the television news there was a close-up of an unrepentant Jones being escorted in and out of court. I saw Adam some time later, and he looked prosperous and happy. We spoke of the affair and he was kind enough not to mention the fact that I thought his claims to be able to pilot a hovercraft were so much bullshit.

He even looked regretful when I said: "It was a good story mate. But if you had driven that craft up through Ryde High Street on a Christmas Day morning, it would have been a great one."

CHAPTER SEVEN

Wet legs, dry wit and a premature death

A TEACHER OF my acquaintance once told me why he had packed up a much better-paid job in a bank to spend his life in the classroom. "Because," he said, "I can always be sure of at least one good laugh a day as a teacher. That was certainly not the case in a bank."

Journalism, at any level, has a similar attraction. The lure of a newsroom has nothing to do with money; provincial hacks, especially, have been poorly-paid for as long as I have been in the profession. Despite this (or perhaps because of it) the profession tends to attract more than its share of eccentrics.

The News at Portsmouth, during the two spells I spent on the newspaper in the seventies and eighties, was certainly not short of an oddball or two. One of them was Charles Green, one of the most pleasant of men who was always a delight to talk to. Except, that is, when he was standing at an adjacent urinal.

Charlie had a tendency (how best to put this?) for riding with no hands. He would stand there at full flow, hands in pockets, whistling happily to himself. It was at this point that talking to him became a hazardous and, for the unwary, a damp business. Charlie was far too polite to speak to anyone without looking at them, so at the slightest hint of conversation he would turn to face its source. He would do so blissfully indifferent to unfinished business elsewhere, and it was not uncommon to see men emerging from the toilet ruefully shaking their trouser-leg.

Another popular member of the staff was Reg Betts, football writer, naval correspondent and bon viveur. It was never wise to engage Reg in conversation about ailments of any kind because whatever you were suffering from he had had it longer, with more spots and at a higher temperature. Having left *The News* for another job, I returned after five years to meet Reg for the first time at the coffee machine. I had forgotten all the lessons I'd learned, and uttered the fateful words: "Hello Reg. How are you?"

Most people would have replied: "I'm fine. And how are you after all this time?"

Not Reg. He turned to face me (we hadn't seen each other for five years remember) and said: "It's as if God said 'where's Britain?' 'where's England?' 'where's Hampshire?' 'where's Droxford?' 'where's Betts?' Cold! Flu!

Bronchitis! Sinusitis! Tonsilitis!" He accompanied each ailment with a downward sweep of his arm, like some deity delivering misery from above. "How am I? That's how I am. Thank you for asking."

Also on the sports desk at that time was boxing, rugby and golf writer Alister Marshall, who hailed from the Scottish Borders, never seemed to be without a smile on his face and had more pals than he knew what to do with. A former player for Hawick and a Scotland B rugby international, Al also possessed the unique ability to eat a cheese and onion roll, drink coffee and smoke a Players untipped all at the same time, often while holding a conversation on the telephone. It was to prove his undoing during what became known on the desk as *A Day in the Death of Billy Streets*.

We were sitting there one morning when Al's phone rang. Soon the air was full of booming sympathy. "Has he really mate?" "Is that right?" "Oh nooo... such a shame." "Still he had a good old innings." "A fine, fine man, one of the best." "Could you give me a few details old mate?"

Al replaced the telephone before announcing: "Old Billy Streets has died. Great chap Billy. I need to bang out an obit if we're going to catch the final edition." A fulsome tribute quickly appeared and former boxer Billy Streets was sent on his way to the great boxing ring in the sky to the accompaniment of some nicely-honed phrases of appreciation from our own correspondent.

The following morning the phone rang. It was the front office. I waited for Al to get a mouthful of cheese and onion roll and take a swig of coffee before I delivered the message. (After all, timing is everything). "There's someone to see you in the front office mate."

"Who?" he asked, taking a drag on his cigarette.

"Billy Streets," I replied.

From the far end of the desk there came a spectacular explosion of breadcrumbs, cheese fragments, coffee and ash. Al was already rehearsing his apologies as he made his way downstairs and all that remained above his chair was a mournful plume of cigarette smoke where a boxing writer had once sat.

When it came to enthusiasm for the job, Big Al's only rival was a chap called Pete Smith the paper's barrel-chested crime correspondent. His list of contacts within the police, ambulance and fire services was legendary. Nothing remotely approaching an emergency happened without Smithy knowing first, and in the unlikely event that someone forgot to give him a ring to warn him of some disaster or police raid, he invariably knew about it anyway because he seemed to spend most of the day and night tuned into the emergency services on his radio.

One day we decided to publish an April Fool's story in which we reported that the previous day (a Sunday) the local police had stopped traffic as it came into Portsmouth and forced drivers to travel the last couple of miles to the cross-channel ferries on the right-hand side of the road to prepare them for driving on the continent. We got the art department to work their magic and they came up with a couple of photos that made it look for all the world as though the cars were driving through the city on the wrong side of the road.

We thought no more about it, but about three months later Smith came into the newsroom tittering wildly. I use the word 'tittering' advisedly because he had a remarkably high-pitched laugh for such a large man. He had in his hand a police house magazine in which it had been reported that the Hampshire Police traffic superintendent based in Winchester had seen our report and issued a severe rollicking to his team in Portsmouth for daring to carry out such a dangerous experiment without first seeking his permission. Few April Fool's stunts work that effectively, and for a time that day Smithy himself was in danger of having to summon one of his mates in the ambulance as he struggled to keep his ribs from splintering.

I have noticed over the years how curmudgeonly people immediately become 'characters' as soon as they've died. One such was Bill Snow, a former chief sub on the *West Sussex Gazette*, whose choleric disposition was partially redeemed by his wit - though it rarely sounded funny to the young reporters on the receiving end.

One young woman who came under his malevolent sphere of influence was delighted to be given the first chance to cover a royal visit to the area, and worked hard to write a 'colour piece.' She had been told that she needed to include some offbeat observations, and was particularly proud to report that 'as the Queen's car passed by Her Majesty looked radiant and showed no signs of her recent catarrh.'

Bill snatched up the telephone as soon as the copy passed across the desk. "Showed no signs of her recent catarrh," he snarled down the line. "What did you expect the woman to do? Gob out the bloody window?"

Bill Snow didn't seem to like anyone very much, but he had a particular antipathy towards young female journalists in general, and one in particular. Indeed, so exasperated had he become with her that he made it known that he would give £50 to anyone who would get her pregnant and therefore out of his professional life.

The woman concerned got to know about this and phoned the old grouch. "Mr Snow," she said, "I understand you have placed £50 on my head."

"It was £50 all right, but it wasn't on your head that I placed it," came the reply.

Bill and printers were not, as a rule, bosom buddies. He regarded them as overpaid artisans and they regarded him as a grumpy dinosaur. Both sides had a point, and neither would waste an opportunity to irritate or embarrass the other.

I recall the day the paste-up department at Portsmouth was brought to a halt as its overseer Trevor Whichello, the most affable of men, slowly paraded through it on the way to Snow's desk. He was swathed in vast quantities of the white bromide paper on which the copy was printed before it was cut up and pasted on to the page by the compositors. It was wrapped round and round his torso and draped over his shoulders and arms. He looked like some semi-mummified Egyptian princess as he shuffled through the newsroom with yards more of the stuff trailing behind him.

Mr Snow had sent out some flower show results to be set in 8pt, which is slightly smaller than the type on the page you are reading at the moment. Instead, he had marked it 80pt, which is about the size of the front-page headline on your average red-top national tabloid. If you bear in mind that this was the largest flower show of the year, that there were classes for everything from miniature gardens on a plate to the longest runner bean, and that the *Chichester Observer* was carrying first, second and third in every class, you will have some idea of the amount of bromide needed to accommodate Mr Snow's error.

Trevor halted his stately progress by the side of Bill's desk and said loud enough for the rest of the room to hear: "Excuse me my good man, but I think we need a bit of a cut on this story." Bill didn't even look up. "Bollocks," he snarled, and once again the tone had been set for the day.

Newspaper offices, like every other place of work, have their share of strange and sad characters. One of the oddest I will call Mildred. She came into my life while I was editor of the *IW Weekly Post*. She walked into the front office one afternoon and asked to see me as a matter of some urgency.

She was a heavy-set woman with a soft voice, but the first thing I noticed about her were her eyes. They were dark and unfathomable and seemed devoid of warmth or character. She said she had been advised to come and see me because she understood we were looking for a part-time copy-inputter. She did not say who had provided her with the information but I remember thinking that whoever it was must have been quick off the mark because we had only made the decision to recruit a couple of hours earlier. Either that, I remember thinking, or this woman must be psychic.

She started with us the following week and wasted no time in getting on the wrong side of my secretary Pat Turner, a brisk, efficient, no-nonsense person who set high standards and expected others to match them. It seems that Mildred was having difficulty concentrating and had began to inform everyone of her interest in spiritualism and the afterlife. Pat would suddenly become aware of a silent typewriter to her left and look round to find Mildred staring vacantly into space and slowly nodding. One of our reporters, Mike Merritt, (mentioned in an earlier chapter) became unhappy at the prospect of working in the same office as Mildred.

"She's bloody weird mate," he would tell me. "Bloody weird. Sometimes I can hear her mumbling to herself and she has this odd smile on her face." Pat, far from being scared, was merely exasperated. "For goodness sake Mildred, do concentrate," she would tell her. Until, that is, Pat came into my office one lunchtime, unusually subdued and carrying a sheet of paper.

"It's Mildred," she said. "You know all this stuff and nonsense about the spirits. Well, this morning she was doing her usual thing of staring into space and smiling when I looked down and noticed she was writing. To be honest, I didn't dare stop her because I didn't know what might happen. But this is what she wrote."

She pushed the piece of paper over to me and there in the most immaculate copper-plate handwriting was a 'message from the other side.' It was enigmatic and flowery, the sort of heavily-embroidered, stilted prose that seems to suit that subject. But it was literate and contained the sort of words and phraseology that Mildred would simply not have been capable of composing without some help from somewhere.

Pat was typically unequivocal. "Look at the quality of the handwriting. Look at the content of what she has written. I'm telling you that I sat and watched her do that. She was staring up at the ceiling the whole time, she didn't once look at what she was writing and the whole process was continuous. I have no wish to be unkind, but you and I both know that she is not capable of work like this without some help from somewhere. It's quite shaken me I must admit."

Nothing more was said, but about a fortnight later Mildred knocked on my door and asked if she could have a confidential word. She asked whether I had ever wondered how she knew about the job vacancy, and I told her I had assumed that she knew someone who knew someone in the office and they had tipped her off.

The mouth smiled but the eyes didn't. "No," she chuckled. "My guide directed me here. I have been sent to tell you that you are an old spirit and that you will not return on many more occasions."

Suddenly, for no more than three or four seconds, her voice dropped a few octaves and became that of a man. Then it returned to normal.

"Did you notice that?" she said. As questions go it was perhaps the most rhetorical I had ever been asked and I was surprised she had not heard my jaw as it dropped on to my desk. "I'm so sorry. My guide gets so impatient sometimes that he will not let me speak for myself. I do apologise on his behalf." I actually heard myself replying: "That's okay. Tell him not to worry."

There then followed a 15-minute conversation between the three of us, in which I discovered that Mildred had first become involved with spiritualism when her son, who had been stillborn, contacted her. It developed from there and she told me she knew precisely when she was going to die. "It will be in my 82nd year," she said.

Sadly, she died a couple of years later while still in her fifties and now 25 years on, I still do not know what to make of Mildred. There is no doubt that she frightened a young reporter, made a very down-to-earth woman think twice and gave me the closest experience I have ever had of somebody who appeared to have strange (if not special) powers.

Another person who drifted into my life for a short time during the *Weekly Post* days was Ronald. He was a hugely intelligent man who had fallen on hard times. He was a former interpreter who liked to hint at his wartime exploits while sipping impressive quantities of cheap sherry in a pub called The Redan in Ryde. He had long since stopped bothering to disguise the shabbiness of his clothes and returned every night to his bedsit in one of the less salubrious parts of the town.

We met when he asked if I would be interested in using the 'bespoke crosswords' that he could supply for 'a modest sum.' At the time, like most provincial newspapers, we were using crosswords from agencies that could provide them for even more modest sums. But Ronald's need (you would never dream of calling him Ron) was greater, so we decided to launch the new crossword with a £1 book token as the weekly prize.

All went well for about six months, when we noticed the remarkable similarity between the handwriting on many of the winning entries. The name and address were different, but the writing was identical. It transpired that Ronald had been using the names and addresses of friends to complete his own crossword and claim the price.

When I tackled him on the matter he looked suitably penitent. "I'm most frightfully sorry old boy," he explained. "But I have a voracious appetite for books and this seemed slightly less seedy than stealing them from a public library. I felt I had earned them in an odd sort of way."

About a year later, Ronald gathered up a couple of bottles of whisky and a bottle of pills and took them back to his lonely bedsit where he ended an existence that had finally become so intolerable that no amount of cheap drink could disguise its anguish. But, to nobody's surprise, he did it in style.

He wrote a long letter personally addressed to the Isle of Wight coroner of the time (a Mr James Bullen), in which he was at pains to point out that he intended to take his life and that he knew exactly what he was doing. Would the coroner be kind enough, therefore, not to record a verdict of suicide while the balance of his mind was disturbed, 'because it isn't. I know exactly what I am doing and why.' He thanked Mr Bullen in advance for his co-operation.

For the first, and only time in my experience, an inquest returned a verdict of suicide, without its customary qualification.

Everyone who knew Ronald was relieved that he had managed to bring a dignified closure to a life, once so rich and full, but which in his view had run its course and was no longer worth living.

CHAPTER EIGHT

A stroll down my favourite Street

I CAN RECALL the moment as it if were yesterday. It was a winter's evening just before Christmas 1960 and I was in the front room watching television alone. Suddenly I heard the first strains of that mournful music that was to become so familiar over the next 40 years. It was accompanied by an urban landscape of smoky chimneys and terraced houses. *Coronation Street* had begun to impose itself upon my consciousness.

Even at the age of 12 I sensed it was something special and called my mother in to watch. We became instant fans and - like millions of others - remain so to this day.

It has always been fashionable to be sniffy about soaps, and over the years there have been plenty that have warranted such disdain. But not *Coronation Street*. Its direction may have wavered alarmingly - especially over the past ten years or so - but the quality of acting and writing has always retained a standard that others have only been able to admire from afar.

My generation never grew up believing that the Street was, as some liked to believe, a realistic drama of life in a small Northern town. We accepted it for what it was, an exquisitely-crafted caricature of such people enhanced by a series of comedy double-acts that have never been surpassed in the history of sustained mainstream television.

Jack and Annie Walker; Annie Walker and Hilda Ogden; Ena Sharples and Minnie Caldwell; Minnie Caldwell and Jed Stone; Hilda and Stan Ogden; Jack and Vera Duckworth; Mavis and Derek; Mavis and Rita; Bet and Alec Gilroy; Reg Holdsworth and Curly Watts, Roy and Hayley Cropper, Norris and Emily - the list may not be endless but it is substantial. Over the years these actors have provided me with more laughs than any other television show with the possible exception of *Only Fools and Horses*.

The Street was in its pomp during the eighties. It was at ease with itself and confident in its ability to serve up a steady diet of comfortable storylines with just the occasional scandal to make the net curtains twitch. It was during this time that I first approached Granada in Manchester with a request to visit the *Coronation Street* set and write a feature. I wasn't particularly concerned whether or not any of the stars would be there; I was more interested in absorbing the ambience of the place. It was a pilgrimage really, to a little dream factory.

At the time the *Coronation Street* set was not the mini theme park it has since become, with thousands of fans traipsing the cobblestones on guided tours every year. It was very much a closed set weith everyone involved fearful of storylines being leaked to the Press and other secrets uncovered. That may seem strange nowadays, when plots are deliberately fed to the newspapers to ensure ever greater viewing figures, but back in the eighties confidentiality was everything.

Eventually I made contact with a chap called John Temple, who was one of the senior producers on the show, and managed to convince him that I was not setting them up to do any form of expose. As a fan of 25 years' standing I merely wanted to indulge myself for a day and write a feature on what it had all been like. He eventually believed me so photographer Murray Sanders and I set off. My pleasure in the day is conveyed in the photographs that appear on pages 130 and 131. Temple immediately recognised a fan when he saw one and was an excellent and relaxed host. Nothing was out of bounds and as we wandered around, two things surprised me.

One was to see how tiny Helen Worth (Gail) and Chris Quinten (Brian) actually are. She wandered by with a friendly smile and he bounced in an enormous fluffy jacket thing and baggy trousers, looking like something that would be produced if Wombles came to know each other in The Biblical sense. The other surprise was to stroll around the end of the road straight on to the set of a London street in Victorian times where the Sherlock Holmes series was being filmed. These things are second nature to those who work in the industry, but such a juxtaposition still comes as a surprise to those of us who don't.

The late Bill Waddington who played Percy Sugden was only too happy to chat about how delighted he was to be enjoying a golden twilight to his career, most of which had been spent slogging around the Northern clubs.

Journalists are reputed (and in some cases almost expected) to be a cynical bunch, and for the most part we are. But we all have those small corners of our souls where we like the magic to linger. It is there that my fondness for *Coronation Street* lives on.

CHAPTER NINE

The Moon man with a loathing of officialdom

SIR PATRICK MOORE is not aware of the fact (and couldn't care less anyway) but he is the only person of note I have met in my journalistic career with whom I have been happy to remain a friend. We first met when I turned up at his West Sussex home to interview him at the beginning of the eighties. He had just written a book on how to thwart and irritate officialdom and had decided to write under the name of RT Fishall.

It was full of tricks like stapling a cheque because it gummed up bank machinery, or deliberately writing a cheque to a public utility for two pence more than was actually required and then making them go to the trouble of writing you a cheque for the excess.

Patrick has always been intolerant when it comes to bureaucrats and the spasm of indignation that eventually led to the book about which we met was ignited when he received a bill from the local gas company. As he himself pointed out, this was fraught with interest from the start since his house had only ever been powered by oil in the 30 years he had lived there.

Whether it was our shared distaste for red tape or our mutual love of cricket I have no idea, but we hit it off from the start and have remained in regular touch for more than 20 years. Earlier this year he finally got round to writing his autobiography, and my review of it below was published in the *Chichester Observer*. It sums up what I think of a man who can, regularly in the course of one conversation, be generous, outrageous, considerate, infuriating and endlessly fascinating.

'THE UFO OF SELSEY'

People who have known Sir Patrick Moore for many years remain tantalised by the man. There is always a suspicion of something more to him than meets the eye (and there is an awful lot that actually meets the eye in the first place!)

For instance, he is reluctant to discuss his childhood in any great detail. Mention of his war record is dismissed with an impatient wave of the hand and is invariably accompanied by the muttered suggestion that he hadn't done anything that anyone in his position wouldn't have done in the same circumstances. He is always anxious to exaggerate his faults and reluctant to acknowledge his generosity.

I have known him for almost 20 years and am aware of the extraordinary lengths to which he has gone to help others without any thought of payment, reward or even thanks. If I were to divulge just one instance here it would probably lead to permanent excommunication from his Selsey home, and that's not a risk worth taking.

However, when he announced that he was going to write his autobiography I was convinced he had constructed a literary trap for himself from which there was to be no escape. At long last, he would have to show us a glimpse of the real Patrick.

Some hopes. The second paragraph of *80 Not Out: The Autobiography*, begins 'I am going to gloss over my first years very briefly.' And he does. In fact, 30 years are dealt with in a little over two pages. He chooses to begin the story proper in 1953, and the details of his strained relationship with his father, his lengthy childhood illness and his exploits in the RAF receive scant attention.

I did, however, learn the name of the love of his life for the first time. She was called Lorna, and the way he writes of her portrays the passions, hatreds and regrets of Patrick Moore in a few poignant paragraphs.

'Lorna, the only girl for me, was no longer around thanks to the activities of the late, unlamented Herr Hitler. Quite recently someone asked me whether she was ever in my mind. I replied that after 60 years there were still rare occasions when I could go a whole half-hour without thinking about her - but not often. This explains why I am a reluctant bachelor and also why I know that if I saw the entire German nation sinking into the sea, I could be relied upon to help push it down.'

Patrick does not give of himself often in this book, so when he does it makes the moment all the more touching. It is certainly an improvement on the first sentence of the book, which reads somewhat unpromisingly: 'On several occasions I have been asked to write an autobiography. I can't imagine why.'

From anyone else it would sound like the gruesome modesty of a famous person who can't wait to tell you all about himself at length. To anyone who knows Patrick, it just sounds like Patrick because we have heard it so many times before.

'Me get a knighthood? What on earth for? What have I done to deserve such a thing? Absolute poppycock! I am an amateur astronomer. Entirely self-taught. Same with music. Picked it up as I went along. Lucky really.'

The implication here is that any child could educate itself to become such an acknowledged expert on another world that they would be sought out to help map the moon for the Apollo landings. The assumption here is that anyone who is not entirely tone deaf could become such a proficient musician that they could also go on to play with the Scottish Symphony Orchestra, write their own marches and operas or compose a piece of music specifically for the wedding of a loved one.

Patrick has done all this and can't understand for a moment what all the fuss is about. He is far happier talking about his prowess as a leg-spinner, his love of seafood, his devotion to his cats and his abhorrence of blood sports.

This is what makes him (in that much over-used phrase) a 'genuine eccentric.' Not for him the affectations of someone who wants to be noticed for the sake of it. The Patrick you see gazing out from the *Sky at Night* studio is the Patrick you meet in the study of his beloved home.

Paradoxically for such an innately private man, he loves company. He is never happier than when his home is thronging with people and he has become a past master at finding excuses to hold a party. Invitations usually state that festivities will begin at noon on a Sunday. They rarely end before midnight and the eclectic mix of people reflects perfectly Patrick's wide variety of interests.

I suspect all of them know some part of Patrick, but few, if any, know the whole man. This means conversation with him is never boring because he will casually toss into the most innocuous exchange a fact which he assumed you already knew. I'll never forget the moment he first mentioned that Brian May, lead guitarist of Queen, was one of his best friends. 'Oh yes, remarkable man. One of the top astrophysicists in the country. An acknowledged expert on cosmic dust you know.'

This side of Patrick Moore forms the backbone of his book. It is a compendium of fascinating facts, outrageous opinions and a willingness to mention some of the famous people he has met only because we expect it of him, and not because he wishes to bask in any reflected glory. He has made it as personal as wants it to be, and that must be the right of any autobiographer.

I have no doubt that the next time we sit down for a chat he will mention some scintillating fact, and as I struggle to return my eyeballs to their sockets he will say: 'Haven't I ever told you that. I'm sure I must have done. Wasn't it in the book?'

I commend everyone to read Patrick Moore's autobiography. You will not find out much about the man himself, but you will certainly be left in no doubt about what the man thinks of the world around him.

CHAPTER TEN

Do they pay you for writing that crap?

I HAVE BEEN writing opinion pieces now for more than 30 years. Whether they wanted to or not, readers have been receiving my views on everything from the non-League football pyramid to nuclear disarmament; from breakfast television to the size of Bounty Bars. Writing regular weekly columns is a privilege. People like me are essentially bar-room philosophers with knobs on. Everyone has opinions, but few are fortunate enough to know that they could be read by well over a million people every week.

The very act of expressing a view on anything means you automatically divide your readers into pros and antis. It also means that they have the right to say what they think about you, and they do so in the most unexpected places. That's all any columnist can ask. If it's true that there's no such thing as bad publicity, then it's equally true to say that if you are a columnist there's no such thing as a bad reaction. "I've never bothered to read it," is far more hurtful than all the bile and calumny in the world.

This doesn't stop critics from having their say, however, and it can be delivered in the most unlikely surroundings. I was standing in a pub urinal one evening when a chap I had never met suddenly asked: "Do they pay you for writing that crap?" Fortunately, it was one of those rare occasions when the perfect response came immediately to mind and was not formed in the early hours of the following morning.

"They certainly do," I replied. "Why? Who reads it to you?"

He did up his zip, stomped out of the latrine and the encounter was over, but I confronted a far more specific example of animosity after a cricket match. The team I was playing for on the Isle of Wight had a fixture against a side from Portsmouth. We agreed to pick them up from the ferry and transport them to the match, which was an agreeable affair. Afterwards we were making arrangements to take them back again, and their captain was allocating different groups to different cars.

He pointed to a group of two men and one woman, and said: "You lot can go back with Keith."

The woman immediately got to her feet and snarled: "What! Go in his car. After what he wrote about Barry Manilow? Not bloody likely!" I rather unchivalrously suggested that she might care to walk instead, as it was a matter of sublime indifference to me one way or the other, but this outburst proved two things. Firstly, that we should always take care about what we write because there is always somebody who takes it more seriously than we might imagine. Secondly, fans of particular performers have long memories, because my less than flattering observations about Mr Manilow had been made more than two years earlier.

It is also easy to be believe that just because you are writing for provincial newspapers your opinions are read only by those in the provinces. Wrong. Companies exist whose function it is to acquire copies of every newspaper in the country and scour them for any references to clients who pay them to act as personal watchdogs. They are called cuttings agencies.

I find it difficult to conceive of the paranoia and egotism that besets such people. Why on earth would anyone want to know what everyone thinks of them all the time? One imagines that the boosts to their self-esteem are balanced out by the slights, so they end up paying a lot of money to discover what we all know anyway. Some people like us, some don't.

I was surprised to receive a personal letter from Cliff Richard a few months after I had written a piece to say that though he was not to my particular taste, I always admired a talent that had been cherished and honed and that I could understand why he had attracted such unquestioning devotion from so many fans over so many years.

He wrote to say that though he did not make a habit of writing to journalists, he would just like to thank me for my kind comments etc. It was a civil if entirely unnecessary thing to have done, but it amounted to someone loved and admired by millions telling someone unknown and unrecognised by even more millions: 'Thank you for not disliking me.' Strange.

I once received a similar letter from Michael Winner, in which he said he found my column 'very jolly.' Unfortunately he never mentioned which column it was and I cannot recall writing one that would have had such an effect upon him.

Max Bygraves went one step further. After reading an article in which I mentioned the fact that anyone who made such limited talent go such a long way and for such a long time had my unbridled admiration, he sent me a copy of his autobiography containing the inscription 'In appreciation Max Bygraves.' It was a wicked thing to do to an innocent journalist, and it was weeks before I dared go near another book.

A creature who has columnists looking fearfully over their shoulder for fear of sudden ambush is the anorak. The person who knows so much about the subject you just happened to have mentioned in passing that he or she come to regard it as their life's mission to further your education. The most extreme example came after I had written about a mini-series called *The Winds of War*, which starred Robert Mitchum and Deborah Kerr.

The romantic denouement came as the leads embraced to a background hum of what I described as Spitfire engines.

This infuriated a retired Wing Commander who wrote: "I do not normally read your articles (all letters of complaint start like that) but last Saturday's regarding *The Winds of War* has been brought to my attention. I should have thought even the most unintelligent journalist - a category into which I have now been obliged to include you - would be able to differentiate between the sound of a Spitfire's Merlin engine and the Pratt and Whitney engine of a Harvard Trainer. In future sir, kindly get your facts right."

The one thing about being a journalist is that you often get the last word, and I wrote to apologise for my oversight adding that "I had always previously prided myself on recognising a Pratt when I heard one." A promising exchange came to an end at this point.

There is an old saying: "Those who can, do. Those who can't, teach." I have always believed that those who can, do, while those who can't, criticise. It is by far the easiest (some might say unworthy) area of journalism. It is, after all, far simpler to tread on a sandcastle than build one.

I wrote a TV column for many years and always felt a bit of a parasite since I was drawing my inspiration from the creative efforts of others. The same applies to all forms of criticism, though the counter argument maintains that people are being paid good money to feature in or produce all manner of art and that their efforts should therefore be open to scrutiny.

Writing about television is the easiest of all since there is so much raw material to chose from, and much of it is sub-standard. People like Clive James elevated scoffing to a fine art, while the rest of us had to be content to bob along in his considerable wake.

Over the past 20 years or so I have written hundreds of opinion columns variously called *Thinking Aloud* or *Something to Say*. At one stage I was churning out three a week and it wasn't a particular hardship because the brief was simple - write about what you like. Canvasses don't come any broader or whiter, and over the years I have taken full advantage of this privilege. Inevitably I have tended to concentrate on the subjects that interest me most - politics, sport, television and nostalgia.

Excavating attics and cupboards to find some of the old ones has taken almost as long as writing this book. I am not, by nature, an organised person so filing away all this stuff neatly has never crossed my mind. I have found most of them stuffed haphazardly in old envelopes or tied up with wool in untidy bundles.

Once a column has been written it belongs to yesterday. I rarely bother to read them in the newspapers on the day of publication, let alone years later. Therefore, when prevailed upon to root them out for the purposes of this book, it was like reading somebody else's work. I had forgotten almost every word, but what was even more fascinating from my point of view was to read once again the views I formed at the time and whether they had been substantiated by later developments.

Not having the gift of prescience, I suppose it works out at about 50-50. Some of the opinions I formed now sound crass, in much the same way as kipper ties and flares now look absurd. But they, like my opinions, were products of their time and seemed quite appropriate. Therefore I have no reason to regret a single word, but that doesn't mean that some of them don't sound rather silly when taken out of context and era.

In the next chapter I have reproduced some of the political columns, and they contain names and events that assumed considerable importance at the time but whose significance has been eclipsed by the passing of the years. In this chapter I have randomly selected some columns of a more personal nature. These, like those in the next chapter, have been faithfully reproduced - though the temptation to tinker with them and make myself appear more intelligent and farsighted was overwhelming.

'HOW TO TELL AN ISLANDER FROM AN OVERNER'

I'm not sure what inspired this little outburst published in The News, *Portsmouth. Probably 40 years of accumulated frustration.*

[SEPTEMBER 1988] - We Isle of Wighters are a pretty tolerant bunch on the whole. It is a characteristic developed from years spent budging up to make room for the millions who wish to spend their summer weeks in our company. However, there is an increasing tendency for Overners to make bogus claims to native status. While we are flattered that so many should wish to claim our heritage as their own, it is becoming necessary to weed out the interlopers. Here are a few foolproof tests to establish the credentials of a true Islander.

You can be sure, for example, that those who take to writing lengthy letters to local newspapers about protecting the beauty of the Island (as though they were the first to notice it and the only ones to care) are of mainland extraction.

On the other hand you may be reasonably certain that the councillors who spend most of their time abusing each other rather than doing the job for which they are elected, are Islanders. They have simply transported their grievances from the playground to the council chamber.

Listen carefully to a resident's terminology. If he calls himself a 'corkhead' he is not a 'caulkhead' and I was once assured that only on the Island are the hands of a clock referred to as 'spears.'

You will rarely see a native Islander on any beach between Ryde and Shanklin during the summer months. These areas are evacuated at the beginning of May and left to the tender mercies of the tourists, while Islanders congregate on the beautiful shores of the West Wight. Any vehicle spotted in Compton

Bay car park during the summer without an Island registration number is regarded as highly suspicious. This massive population shift is probably one of the reasons the Military Road is falling into the sea.

You will never hear a real Islander ask: 'Have you ever been to Blackgang Chine?' All Islanders go there at least once a year because they know that pound for pound it is probably the best value holiday attraction in Britain.

Islanders have several unmistakable physical traits. For example, they have flat skulls acquired from years of banging their head on the roof of their car while travelling on local roads, the surfaces of which are best described as lunar. In the past rescue parties have been despatched to the Ryde-Shanklin road to retrieve Robin Reliant drivers whose entire vehicles have disappeared down potholes.

If you see an Island motorist tottering uncertainly from his car he is rarely drunk, merely giddy from swerving in and out of craters on the main thoroughfares. Brawny excavators from the gas, electricity and water boards do their bit to ensure that any journey between Ryde and Newport is like an audition for *The Krypton Factor*. If you see a motorist smiling you can be sure he owns either a tyre or replacement windscreen business on the Island.

The County Surveyor is thought to be the only one in the country with a degree in potholing, and the traffic flow on the outskirts on Newport every morning and evening, so ingeniously planned and so impossible to navigate, should lead to the area being renamed Rubik's Roundabout.

Genuine Islanders are always round-shouldered. This deformity has evolved from the generations who have spent many years huddled against the elements at the end of Ryde Pier. A comparatively recent native affliction is writer's cramp, brought on from filling in endless Sealink questionnaires.

Always check an Islander's tongue. The genuine article will be heavily pock-marked from years of being bitten while its owner has had to listen to mainlanders who choose to move to the Island to live 'because it is different' and then complain because there is not a Marks and Spencer on every corner.

Eyes are another natural giveaway. In an Islander they roll easily to the top of the head in weary resignation, thought to be caused by having to listen to variations on the following themes. 'Do you get duty free on the ferries?' 'Have you got a passport?' 'Are you getting used to electricity over there now?'

Yes, we Islanders are a pretty tolerant bunch on the whole.

'SWEET SHOPS THAT LEAVE SUCH A BITTER TASTE'

This reminiscence was inspired by a visit to a soulless supermarket with my daughter Sam, who was six years old at the time.

[JULY 1987] - Wandering around a chain store with my daughter on Saturday I despaired at how depressingly sanitary and organised the confectionery section has become. The fragrant, ramshackle delights of the old-fashioned sweet shop seem to have disappeared and as a result an important piece of her childhood is being legislated out of existence.

A battery of containers was on display and each plastic jar was neatly labelled with a large sign proudly proclaiming the absence of harmful additives therein. Also absent was the equally harmful price. Each bulging receptacle was accompanied by a little shovel, which children were being urged to use 'in the interests of hygiene.' They actually use them in the interests of the shop's profit, ladling vast quantities of goodies into paper bags, which parents are then prevailed upon to pay for when it is too late to turn back.

It is a brave man or woman who holds up the inexorable progress of a check-out queue to return a handful of pony-shaped fruit jellies.

It is not the cynical, market-orientated, sales-targeted exploitation I object to, but the fact that some of the stardust of childhood, already spread perilously thin, is being swept away. When I was a little'un, back in the days before bacteria had been invented, a trip to the sweetshop at the end of our street was a fine adventure. It was a lingering pleasure, during which the destiny of every old penny was discussed. Was it going to provide four Blackjacks, four Fruit Salads, two gobstoppers or four of those pink shrimp things that used to stick to the roof of your mouth like putty on a coconut mat?

Perhaps you would opt instead for eight aniseed balls (I love them to this day), one vast pink wodge of bubblegum or a sliver of chewing gum which had the taste and consistency of damp cardboard and came wrapped in an obscure American cartoon. All these delights - and many more besides - like sweet cigarettes, sweet tobacco and liquorice pipes with a silly red button - were located in a dim corner of the shop.

Once selected they were taken to the counter where Mr Culverhouse would proceed to fashion a cone-like container out of newspaper and drop them in, counting as he went. 'Ha'penny... penny... tuppence... thruppence... no, you can't have it for nothing just because the wrapper's come undone... thruppence ha'penny... fourpence the lot.'

On those rash occasions when you decided to blow your entire fortune on a quarter of sweets from the posh jars on the top shelf, you still received the same treatment from Mr Culverhouse and his homemade container which the previous day had been a copy of the *Daily Sketch*.

Strange things began to happen to sticky sweets left overnight. They began to take on some of the content of the newspaper in which they were wrapped, and my prize possession for several days was a sherbert lemon with half of Nat Lofthouse's face imprinted on the side. I showed it all around the school playground and it was regarded with the reverence of the Turin Shroud.

Another favourite, now long gone, was lemonade powder. Added to water it made undrinkable lemonade but a bag of the stuff in your jacket pocket was perfect for dipping into during lessons. It offered the possibility of silent consumption and was undetectable save for the tell-tale bright yellow stain on your forefinger at the end of the day.

One of the endearing traits of childhood is gullibility and boundless optimism. You always think your packet of fruit gums will have more red ones than anyone else's, or that yours will be the first sherbert fountain in history not to clog up after one suck.

One firm relied upon this ingenuousness to perpetrate upon my generation the greatest confectionery scam of them all - the Jamboree Bag. These were like cheap crackers, minus the bang. They promised much and delivered little. Time after time high anticipation dissipated into sullen disillusionment as the meagre contents revealed themselves.

Four pence (the equivalent of 16 Blackjacks don't forget) usually provided a paltry yield of a plastic toy, a lollipop of indeterminate colour and flavour and what appeared to a selection of reject dolly mixtures. I can still feel the flatness of the moment to this day. But we still went back for more.

'THE POISON PEN LETTERS THAT I ALWAYS TREASURE'

Part of the fun of writing opinion pieces is that there are plenty of readers who do not share the sentiments expressed therein. This often results in a merry exchange of correspondence when people have the courage to include their name and address (alas, most don't). This article was written after I had spent some time reading my 'fan mail.' The 'Bell' referred to is Betty Bell, who in those days was a doughty fighter on behalf of the residents of what is said to be Europe's largest council estate, Leigh Park near Havant.

[DECEMBER 1987] - It is possible to gauge the success of a writing year by the number of anonymous letters that find their way on to my desk. They are usually abusive, of course, and therefore greatly treasured. I receive relatively few of the 'Dear Moron' variety. My detractors are altogether more inventive, going to considerable trouble to package their venom. One cannot help but be flattered.

For example, those who consider me to be to the right of Monsieur Le Pen will no doubt be shattered to learn that I regularly receive snotty little postcards from one of the National Front's leading proponents locally. He fondly believes them to be anonymous because he doesn't sign his name, but I happen to edit readers' letters from time to time and I recognise the typewriting.

I had almost given up hope of hearing from him this year, but my gall in criticising Mike Gatting sent vibrations down into the woodwork and our friend came tumbling out a fortnight ago. The style is instantly recognisable.

Buff envelope, ancient typewriter (black ribbon) and a plain postcard inside on to which the legend of the moment is committed.

He first made his appearance a year or two back with the rather limp observation that 'there are no two greater spivs than Newbery and Bell.' As the Bell in question was Betty of Leigh Park fame, I considered myself to be in esteemed company. There was an added refinement on the latest offering. The logo at the top of this column had been neatly cut out and attached to the postcard (that's another paper sold, thank you) and written above it were the words: 'Look in the mirror and you will see **** in human form.'

The asterisks are there to prevent this column acquiring a Channel Four-type reputation, but for the benefit of those with limited imaginations suffice it to say that if you were to spread me on your roses the result would be blooms of surpassing loveliness.

The consensus of opinion within the office was that such a description could only have come from someone who knows me well. However, someone who knows me not at all is the religious nutter who keeps sending enigmatic pronouncements through the post. The latest to arrive is a huge poster of autumn leaves, printed upon which is a quotation from John 11:25 which reads: 'Jesus said: "He who believes in me, though he dies yet shall he live."' Stuck above that is the Thinking Aloud logo (that's another one sold, thank you again) which leads me to believe that weirdos who shelter beneath anonymity also have a cut and paste fixation.

In with the poster was a tiny leaflet giving a few tips on how we sinners can get to know God. I can only assume from the gist of the poster and the leaflet that the sender does not consider I have so far made any effort to establish a celestial rapport myself. Be that as it may, I know enough to assure myself that the Holy Spirit does not reside within those who choose to flaunt their self-perceived goodness and are so lacking in moral courage that they consider it their mission in life to clutter my letterbox with unattributed piety.

I place this sort of 'Christian' in the same category as a woman I spotted on the Cowes-Southampton ferry recently. Throughout the journey she had her face buried in a hymnbook, which seemed to induce in her the same catatonic trance as that inflicted on the youth of today by personal stereos.

Her only contact with the outside world came through her scowling relationship with the unfortunate gentleman at her side whom I took to be her husband. He danced attendance on her throughout the trip, plying her with tea, biscuits etc. He even straightened the large cross she wore around her neck. He was rewarded with a withering glance if he was lucky, but not one please or thank you emanated from the general direction of the hymnbook.

Two youngsters playing with a soft toy on wheels twice inadvertently let it stray in the general direction of the woman's feet. The subsequent 'tut' sounded like a plunger being wrenched from a blocked sink. A grim impenetrable mist seemed to surround the woman. A sense of self-righteousness throbbed through her. Like so many of her kind, she was giving religion a bad name.

'SCOOTERISTS SHOW THEIR TRUE COLOURS'

This column referred to another spat, this time with a group of stunningly illiterate scooter riders who took exception to my criticism of their holiday antics on the Isle of Wight during the summer of 1988.

[JUNE 1988] - Three months ago I wrote an article about the thousands of scooterists who invade the Isle of Wight every year. The tone (I referred to them as 'scooterus scruffuli') was not particularly complimentary, nor was it intended to be.

The reaction was immediate. A Latin student from Southsea wrote to point out that I had employed the wrong tense throughout the piece. Then it all went quiet except for a letter (anonymous of course) from somebody who said the article in question had been forwarded to a publication called *Scootering* Magazine (I look forward to receiving the cheque) and that when it was printed 'you had better watch out pal, because you will be a marked man.'

Three months have since passed and I am now in a position to impart some good news to *Scootering* Magazine. It has at least 11 readers, for that is the number who have written to complain about the piece, with varying degrees of literacy.

Most of them abusively maintain that they are paragons of society, like Allen Hall of Hinkley who wrote (and I quote verbatim): 'I am making an offical complant about one of your journalist's who goes by the name of Kieth Newberry. After reading one of his articals about a certain scooter run, who the hell does the shirt lifter think his is? Sorry, but I take it very personal.'

Somebody else to take it personal was Mr G Fletcher of Sidcup who is not a man given to compromise or conciliation. 'I can assure you,' he wrote, 'that you can write all you like and we will keep riding our scooters to the Isle of Wight or anywhere else. I wrote this not from blind hatred but just to let you know that you as a man and a local rag are just one of thousands of little thorns in our side which appear every year.'

I wonder whether G Fletcher has ever stopped to consider why he and his kind attract so many 'thorns' in the course of 12 months?

He concludes: 'To us you are just a petty little man with a big chip on your shoulder, trying to use pathetic slanderous articles to stir up yet more trouble against scootering. I have refrained from using foul language and hope you read this if only you might learn something.'

There were angry little missives from Mr AS White of Ripon and Ms J Britten of Burton-on-Trent among others, but the most articulate response came from Miss D Howe of Pinner. She began by making the assertion that I had never met her (right), or her friends (right) or probably any scooterist at all (wrong). I can only point out to Miss Howe that when you live on the Isle of Wight as I do, and Easter descends, it is impossible not to meet more scooterists in a day than one would wish to meet in a lifetime.

Miss Howe's main bone of contention is my reference to the 127 arrests made at last Easter's rally. She points out that some arrests were made for 'minor offences' and that the 127 concerned 'were not rampaging drunkenly through the streets of the Island raping and pillaging on their way.'

Everyone who has written has been mortified at the thought that anyone should regard them as scruffy or yobbish, and this came as no surprise. I did not actually expect anyone to write: 'Dear Sir. Ref your article of April 5th. I was among those who threw up on the pavement, flopped drunkenly under a hedge, left my litter in the streets and rode my unsilenced scooter at speed through the streets of Sandown in the middle of the night.'

However, all these correspondents are deluding themselves if they believe such anti-social activities did not occur during the course of that weekend. They would also be doing themselves and us a favour by publicly condemning such behaviour and not seek to defend it by writing letters of outrage.

PS: If anyone feels the urge to send this article to *Scootering* Magazine, tell them they can use it free of charge.

'BOXING DOESN'T DESERVE BRUNO'

Back in the eighties British sport produced two unlikely heroes in Eddie 'The Eagle' Edwards and Frank Bruno. In these two columns I forecast that one would have difficulty in coping with the aftermath of fame, while the other seemed perfectly positioned to do so. These predictions proved to be spot on - except that I got the people the wrong way round. It just goes to show how wrong you can be.

[JUNE 1988] - Boxing desperately needs Frank Bruno, but it certainly does not deserve him. His simple dignity is one of the few redeeming factors about a sport which, in the last quarter of a century, has allowed itself to become sleaze-ridden and corrupt. It is foolish to pretend that professional boxing has ever been anything other than brutal and mercenary, but there was also a time when it was also possessed of a cruel nobility. It was sport in which savagery and respect were comfortable bedfellows. Then the sharks moved in.

Their influence is best exemplified by the MC's cry which heralds so many title fights these days. 'For the undisputed championship of the world...'

In my youth nobody disputed the undisputed nature of a title fight. There was one world authority, eight weights and eight world champions. Everyone knew where they stood or fell and world championship bouts, like Test matches, were precious occasions.

With the increased sophistication of pan-world communications, it did not take the unscrupulous long to realise that if you had more weights and more champions, you had more title fights and made more money. From that point, professional boxing became cheapened and degraded. Sports columns became infested with meaningless initials. At any given weight it was likely that the WBC champion was not only different from the WBA champion, he probably came from a separate continent entirely. At the time of going to print there were two other world authorities with more to come no doubt.

Four separate authorities was bewildering enough, but the moneymen then compounded the confusion by inventing new weight categories. Unknowns were suddenly introduced as world light middleweight champions in a sport where a light middleweight had previously been called a welter-weight.

With the market having been successfully expanded, the exploitation began in earnest. In the pre-Tyson era, the four 'undisputed world heavy-weight champions' all made a handsome living by successfully avoiding each other. Then along came Don King with an elaborate and lucrative scheme for, as he once put it, 'reunifying' the heavyweight division. It was tantamount to a vandal smashing a valuable piece of porcelain and then demanding an extortionate fee for putting it back together again.

It was from this muscular maelstrom that Mike Tyson emerged, bull-necked and fearsome. King waited for the young man to destroy everything in his path and then, with his uncanny gift for making the most of other people's gifts, he stepped in. For a man of such awesome power, Tyson is strangely vulnerable. Like most young sporting champions, he has now got everything he needs but he doesn't need everything he's got - and that includes Mr King.

This is the predicament that came under the accurate scrutiny of Bruno's girlfriend Laura, after the fight. She said: 'If Tyson had walked out of that ring a loser he would have had nobody because he is not loved like Frank.'

These were not the hysterical ramblings of a bad loser but the perceptive observations of a woman who is determined that the man she loves will never be reduced to a statistic in a sport where some men must be casualties if other men are to be crowned. You get the impression that if Muhammad Ali had had someone like Laura Mooney at his side during the great years he would not now be reduced to a shuffling hulk; a battered old trophy to be dusted off and put on show every few months.

It is the stability of his domestic arrangements that makes Frank Bruno a serene figure in a violent world. And it is that serenity that will always prevent him from becoming the heavyweight champion of the world. A nasty man can always pretend to be nice, but in the unforgiving environs of professional boxing it is impossible for a nice man to pretend to be nasty. The sham is soon exposed. All this will mean little to Bruno as he struggles to muster a smile in the sour aftermath of defeat, but the ultimate triumph is his.

After the fight, Tyson returned to a mansion, a pile of money and the clamour of empty admiration. Bruno returned to the genuine love and affection of his family and an eternal place in the affections of a nation. Ten years from now Mike Tyson will give everything to be able to swap places with the man he clubbed into submission last weekend.

'HOW WILL EDDIE COPE WHEN THE LAUGHTER'S OVER?'

[MARCH 1988] - In the last week or so, on the other side of the world, two Britons from opposite ends of the social spectrum have been making something of an impression. One is being callously used by the system and the other is using the system for all she is worth.

First let us deal with the victim - Eddie 'The Eagle' Edwards - a man whose very name will induce a weary sigh whenever it is mentioned a few months from now. He is the latest example of the kind of popular flotsam periodically picked up on the tide of public adulation, then left stranded when it ebbs away. Characters as diverse as Simon Dee and Tiny Tim have been beached in similar fashion. The secret is to make as much as you can while the water is still high and flowing in your direction.

It is easy to see the appeal of Edwards. He is indefatigable, chirpy, affable, unpretentious and courageous. If the cinema is to be believed, characters like him won the last war for Britain as they gazed defiantly skywards from amid the rubble of a broken city.

He owes his fame to this and the fact that Canadians and Americans had so few successes to cheer at the Winter Olympics that they did the next best thing and supported our failures. With a push here and a prod there it is possible for approval to become enthusiasm, for enthusiasm to become acclaim and for acclaim to become irrational worship.

At this point two things inevitably occur - the marketing men move in and the media, who have fuelled the hype, then begin the debunking process. Alistair Burnet, for example, was decidedly sniffy when featuring Edwards' self-conscious foray into the world of popular music on *News at Ten*. The Burnet mouth set like a rat-trap and the eyes took on a cynical glaze. 'His critics call him Eddie the Emu, and emus can't sing either,' said the sage of ITN with a line as unfunny as it was uncalled for.

At the moment Edwards is poised to gather in the bounty from his incompetence and I wish him well. I also hope he proves strong enough to withstand the sense of disillusionment and betrayal he is certain to feel when public interest wanes in a fifth-rate ski-jumper, as it is bound to before long.

Someone who committed herself to a lifetime in the spotlight was Miss Sarah Ferguson when she agreed to marry Prince Andrew. It must be said that she shows no signs of regretting that decision, though the same cannot be said for the rest of the country. I have long harboured the notion that the Duchess of York regards membership of the Royal Family as a season ticket for a sponsored jolly, and nothing she has said or done in the past 12 months has convinced me otherwise.

During that time she has managed to arrange - at no great expense to herself - trips to Mauritius, Antigua, France, Canada, New York and now Los Angeles. She is about to embark on her third ski-ing holiday in eight weeks and it is about time somone applied a brake to this particular gravy-train. This sybaritic approach to life is compounded by her general demeanour, which she probably believes to be the common touch but which actually comes across as a touch common.

Like most people in this country, I have been an instinctive Royalist for as long as I can remember, but that affection has always been based on respect. However, that respect is not remotely enhanced by the sight of a duchess gallumphing around the world at our expense, indulging in nudge-nudge, wink-wink repartee with the luminaries of Hollywood or prancing around in a £5,000 dress jabbing an umbrella point into unsuspecting buttocks in the Royal enclosure at Ascot.

Being a member of the Royal Family brings with it privilege and status, but it demands far more, like elegance, commitment, poise and service to others. These are not qualities one automatically associates with the Duchess of York.

I sense rumblings of disapproval about her behaviour that could easily develop into something far more damaging. Now is the appropriate time for somebody to explain to her that membership of the House of Windsor does not entitle her to act like a Sloan Square Redcoat.

'RETROSPECTIVE ON THIS GAME OF FORECASTING'

It is only when you delve through a bunch of cuttings that you begin to realise how certain people and/or subjects become something of a fixation. A topic I returned to on more than one occasion over the years was weather forecasters and their ineptitude. My faith in them was not exactly strengthened when Michael Fish failed to notice a hurricane that was careering through the western approaches and actually fluttering his trouser legs while he was busy refusing to acknowledge its existence.

[JANUARY 1987] - I have a friend who is congenitally unpunctual. For as long as I have known him he has regarded arriving on time as a personal weakness. Yet he insists on having his digital watch correct to the second.

Questioned on this apparent contradiction he will say in all seriousness: 'I always like to know precisely how late I am.'

I suspect a similar attitude exists among those who study weather forecasts every night on all four channels in order that next day they are in a position to know precisely how inaccurate they all were. You can always tell a meteoromaniac because they become indoctrinated in the jargon of weather forecasting. Soggy bus shelters through Lincolnshire echo with their rueful observations. 'I thought this front was supposed to be deepening in the Irish Sea and skirting the Welsh coast before heading slowly north,' they say to nobody in particular.

Graduates from the Francis Wilson School of Homemade Cliches can be recognised instantly. They talk about rain clouds 'pulsing' across the country, bringing some 'spits 'n' spots' which could well develop into 'thorms.'

Those brought up with Michael Fish as their mentor wear ghastly ties, smack their lips a lot and insist that rain will be found 'more especially' in the east before it drifts south where it will be noticed 'more especially' along 'an imaginary line joining Dorset and The Wash.' The Ian McCaskill influence can be detected in those who make silly little jokes while a thunder cloud hurries along in their direction.

Indeed, the English are now so dependent upon wayward weather forecasts as part of their staple conversational diet they have lost sight of how appallingly unreliable they have actually become. It was hoped that computers and satellites would help the situation and they have made one important difference. The forecasts are now technologically imprecise; the blunders we now witness every night are now far more reliable because they are made by computers and blessed by scientists.

In order to shroud their incompetence weathermen now weave a subtle thread of hindsight into their performance whenever possible. The country's hottest, wettest and coldest areas are regularly identified and noted, but we are never told whether the people living there were informed in advance that their communities would be particularly sweltering, drenched or glacial.

Anyway, we all know what the weather was like yesterday. What we really require is some approximation of what it will be like tomorrow. But more than ever this is becoming a forlorn hope.

There is always one sure sign that a nation is becoming disaffected with its professional meteorologists - the purveyors of folklore come into their own. One of the most technologically sophisticated countries in the world begins to study the density of frog-spawn to find out where its next sunny day is coming from.

Reporters from television and the national Press descend upon countryside crackpots who believe they can foretell the weather from the angle of a swallow's tail or the frequency with which woodlice mate. So far as I am able to tell, neither hedgehogs nor hawthorn bushes are blessed with foresight. They merely react to the ill-predicted elements that happen to be raging around them at the time.

But back to the professionals for a moment. How much longer are we expected to take seriously men who inform us that one side of the country will have bright periods and scattered showers, while the other will have intermittent rain and some sunshine? You will often hear or read interviews with Messrs Fish, Wilson, McCaskill et al in which they lament the fact that 'people seem to blame us if the weather is bad.' Nonsense, gentlemen. People blame you because you didn't tell them it was going to be bad. Or because it was bad when you told them it was going to be good.

By any standards of analysis or quality control, British weather forecasting is shoddy. And in most cases human nature is to blame, not Mother Nature.

'SOMETHING FISHY ABOUT THESE FOUL WEATHER BLASTS'

[OCTOBER 1987] - *Dateline: Isle of Wight, Thursday, 13.30 hours.* I am watching television. Weatherman, Michael Fish, smirks at the camera. "A woman rang to say she heard there was a hurricane on the way. Well she needn't worry, there isn't."

Dateline: Isle of Wight, Friday, 02.30 hours. The non-existent hurricane is centred directly over our house. Is that the pitter-patter of rain I hear? No, it's the pitter-patter of slates dropping on to the garden path.

06.30 hours: A neighbour, successfully avoiding low-flying oak trees, is attempting to get his car out of the garage. First he has to get his garage out of the car.

07.00 hours: I switch on the bedside lamp and the gloom in the room remains. The electricity, like a quarter of the roof, is down. We immediately ring neighbours to ensure they are equally badly off.

Jim the newsagent is bemoaning the unscheduled take-off time of his new larchwood fence, last seen soaring above the Solent. "At least you've still got the trees you planted immediately behind it," says my wife.

"Did have," says Jim

08.00 hours: Breakfast is over. It's surprising how tasty Coca Cola and a Penguin can taste at this time of the morning. Time to go outside and survey the carnage. You've heard of a night on the tiles? Well, this was a morning on the slates. We pick our way along the path, shielding our eyes from unaccustomed shafts of light beaming through gaps where fence panels once stood.

We check the post. There are no letters. Come to think of it, there is no letter-box either.

11.00 hours: The builder arrives to carry out a post mortem on the departed tiles. He becomes quite misty-eyed because it was only a couple of months ago he tenderly placed them aloft during a complete re-roofing job.

"They were so young," he murmurs.

Suddenly his eyes darken. "It's not just your tiles mate, part of your roof has actually shifted. Better let the insurance know." I ring the Nationwide. "Roof is it?" asks a weary voice. "Okay, we'll send you a claim form."

"Actually it could be structural damage..."

The ensuing 15 seconds consist of various aahhs, ohs and ums, ending with: "Of course, that's different all together." Was he suggesting this structural damage was nothing to do with the elements and had occurred, purely coincidentally, after the strongest recorded winds for 284 years?

He couldn't say at this stage sir, but he would be sending a form and we could expect a visitation from an assessor 'eventually.'

19.00 hours: Still no electricity, but the street lights are on. They must be on a different circuit.

20.00 hours: The entire family goes to bed. Strange how unappealing life can be when you're wrapped in a duvet, cuddling a glass of Fanta orangeade, and listening to John Pardoe on *Any Questions*.

Dateline: Isle of Wight, Saturday, 06.00 hours: Still no electricity, but there is a warm glow emanating from the neighbours. "They must have exceptionally good oil lamps," observes my wife.

13.00 hours: Still no electricity. On a whim I decide to see if the trip switch is off. It is. I switch it on and the house thrums back to life. Confirmation from a neighbour that power had been restored the previous evening at about the same time we were enduring *Friday Night is Music Night* on our tinny transistor while devouring bags of Monster Munch.

14.00 hours: I pick up the newspapers. Leader writers are asking, without exception: 'Why didn't the weathermen warn us?'

Michael Fish is quoted as saying: 'The lady who rang in about the hurricane is from Wales, and Wales was not affected. Anyway, it wasn't a hurricane, only a very deep depression, so technically I was correct.'

I am going outside now to find Michael Fish, and I may be gone some time...

'SEARCH FOR THE ELUSIVE WATER PIPES'

[NOVEMBER 1987] - "Water pipes is elusive things." I know this to be true because the man looking for them in our back garden told me so. I had always imagined water pipes to be hulking great things through which gallons flowed and gurgled every minute. The thought that they might be difficult to detect had never crossed my mind.

Their whereabouts on the Isle of Wight had suddenly assumed a crucial importance to the Southern Water Authority, because Islanders are being used as national guinea pigs in the metering campaign. We are in the vanguard of the 'pay as you flush' movement.

The problems began when the advance party from the water authority arrived in a van bearing the uncompromising legend 'Corgi gas installers.' They were also a day late, so confidence was not at its highest.

They were encountering what is known in American politics as 'real problems.' Not only could they not find the appropriate water pipes in the village, they were having considerable difficulty finding some of the houses the pipes were intended to serve.

They bore with them the Isle of Wight's equivalent of the *Mappa Mundi*, an ancient parchment upon which long-defunct farms were strongly featured. Areas depicted as gardens now had cute little bungalows covering them. Much head-scratching was starting to take place.

"This lot don't make our job no easier," said one of the men, gazing vexatiously at the lane under which he was fairly certain our water supply happily cascaded. But surely they had been provided with up-to-date diagrams showing the exact location of the pipes? "Nah," said the man, reaching ominously for a metal detector which he proceeded to waft hopefully over a patch of tarmac.

Just when one suspected a water divining rod was about to be produced from the bowels of the gas van, his eyes lit up. He thought he was getting a bit of a reading. At this point our neighbour arrived on the scene. She is a doughty lady around whom, it always appears, the entire village was constructed. She immediately began to shed some light upon the *Mappa Mundi*.

"That's a laugh, that nursery hasn't been there for ages... there has been a bungalow on that garden for more than 20 years... what's this space all about, there's a road there now." The men looked suitably betrayed and squirmed uncomfortably within their vivid yellow waterproof jackets.

Our neighbour then proceeded to inform the experts where she thought they would find the concealed pipe. They made grateful noises, left, returned with a far more sophisticated metal detector and discovered the pipe about six inches from where she had indicated.

Our meter, due to be installed on December 12 (or thereabouts) will be positioned just outside the gate. Obvious question number one. 'Why not inside or immediately adjacent to the home, where it might conceivably be safer?' They answered in the weary but polite tone adopted by people accustomed to answering the same question a hundred times in the past and certain they will be asked it a thousand times in the future. Apparently this placement is to make the job of the meter-reader easier. Our convenience does not come into it.

Obvious question number two. 'I suppose our water will cost us more in the long term?' I was greeted with an 'are you mad' smile. As far as meters are concerned, it is a clear case of ask not what your water authority can do for you, rather ask what you can do for your water authority.

Obvious question number three. 'What is the going rate for water these days?' It is about 50p per cubic metre. For the benefit of those people, including me, who find it impossible to imagine water in cubes (we always called it ice) it works out at about 50p per 220 gallons. Based on this rate, I have prepared a rough tariff of everyday ablutions and requirements.

One bath - 1.7p; one shower - 0.8p; one toilet flush - 0.2p; one glass of water - 0.01p; one washing-up - 0.66p. All this looks seductively inexpensive, but the only people likely to benefit are the great unmarried, the great unwashed and people with a pathological dislike of gardening and car cleaning.

Meanwhile the purveyors of water butts in the Isle of Wight hinterland are understood to be doing brisk business.

CHAPTER ELEVEN

Politics - The most amusing show on earth

I HAVE ALWAYS had a consuming interest in politics, or rather the performance of politics. Whether it takes place in the cockpit at Westminster or the studios of *Newsnight* it has been compulsive viewing for as long as I can remember. It is human drama in its rawest form and party conferences were 'reality TV' before the phrase took on its rather tiresome contemporary connotations. But when I close my eyes and think politics, it is people rather than policies that spring to mind.

There's Derek Hatton's petulant little face contorted by sweat and hatred as Neil Kinnock took him on at the Labour conference. There's John Nott's truculent little pout before he snatched the microphone from around his neck and walked out on an interview with Robin Day.

There's Edward Heath's thundercloud of an expression when Margaret Thatcher dragged him up on to the stage to endure a sitting ovation at her first conference as Conservative leader. There's George Brown's bibulous grin as he bandied gentle insults with Robin Day during an election broadcast back in the sixties.

The politician I have most enjoyed meeting is Mo Mowlam. I interviewed her in front of an audience of about 400 in a Chichester church when she was on a promotional tour for her autobiography. We met in an ante-room of the church and went for a stroll in the gardens. We hit it off straightaway (it's impossible to dislike her) and the name of Peter Mandelson eventually made its way into the conversation.

I asked her what she thought of him. She paused for a moment and said: "Are these gardens consecrated? Are they actually part of the church do you know?" I told her I didn't think they were. She then proceeded to describe her erstwhile cabinet colleague in most unecclesiastical terms.

I took my place on the little stage in the church and it was agreed that I would introduce Mo and she would walk from the back of the room up to the stage. I thought I would do the show-bizzy thing of walking down to welcome her with a kiss. As I lowered my head to hers she whispered: "No tongues dear. No tongues."

Of the others I have met, James Callaghan was a disappointment. He seemed permanently on the defensive and was reluctant to acknowledge, far less discuss his Portsmouth childhood, which, for someone representing a Portsmouth newspaper, was a little frustrating.

I had a five-minute conversation with Margaret Thatcher when she was on the campaign trail in 1979. We were introduced in a Conservative club thronging with her supporters and I was to understand immediately what they meant when they said she had no time for small talk. "I'm told you launched a weekly newspaper on the Isle of Wight a few years ago. Tell me, where did you acquire the funding? How many jobs have you created? Where do you intend to take it from here?"

She stared directly into my eyes throughout the interrogation (for that is what it was) listened to every reply I gave her and immediately used it as a launch-pad for her next line of inquiry. I felt I had been put through an intellectual mangle and after a few minutes there wasn't a drop of conversational moisture left in me. I had been wrung dry.

From that moment on it was possible for me - against all the odds - to feel sorry for people like Neil Kinnock, Michael Heseltine, Ronald Reagan, Mikhail Gorbachev and any passing French or German leader who wandered within range. They never had a chance, and no matter how history goes on to judge Margaret Thatcher, those who have actually met her (albeit in a smoky bar for a few minutes) will know what a mighty intellect lurked beneath that Barbara Cartland bouffant.

I have reprinted a few political columns I wrote in the eighties. They have been chosen at random except for the fact that I have tried to feature characters from all the main parties. Again, it was sorely tempting to tweak them and give myself a reputation for far-sightedness that I don't deserve. But by leaving them as they were written, it shows what I was thinking at the time and how wrong some people can be.

'WARM GREETINGS TO OLD FOLK FROM AUNTIE EDWINA'

[NOVEMBER 1987] - Following her well-received speech in Reading last week, Junior Health Minister, Mrs Edwina Currie, has prepared an advice sheet to help the elderly survive the coming winter. A copy has been leaked to me. It reads:

Hello all you lovely white-haired cuddly little people. You will notice I have refrained from addressing you as 'pensioners' because I find the term frightfully patronising. I am sure you, in your own quaint, old-fashioned way, do as well.

I realise education has moved on apace since your schooldays, so in case you are not sure what 'patronising' means, it is a condescending attitude adopted by people who regard themselves as superior in every way to those they are addressing. And we are not having any of that nonsense are we, my little wrinklies?

Now then, it won't be long before Jack Frost is tapping at the window pane, so we have to make sure the nasty fellow doesn't get in don't we?

It may have crossed your minds as you toddle down the road for your hard-earned pensions each week that the easiest thing would be for the Government to ensure that you have all the fuel you need to ensure your lovely little homes stay warm and cosy, without having to worry about the cost. However, there are two teensy things wrong with this solution.

Firstly it would cost Mrs Thatcher lots of pennies, but more importantly we in Government know how proud you all are, and quite rightly so, at being the generation which fought to keep this country free. We would not wish to insult all you marvellous people by treating you as a special case. Indeed, it is my intention to bring back memories of those wonderful wartime days - like misery, deprivation, fear, cold and darkness. Won't it be fun as we work together once more to make Britain a happier place in which to live?

That's why I want you all to get out those knitting needles. "But I can't knit," I hear some of you cry. "I suffer from arthritis or rheumatism." Well we won't let little things like that stop us will we? All we have to do is go out and buy a knitting machine. They are not expensive - you can get one for as little as £500 - and they are frightfully good fun to play with.

First of all I suggest you knit a nice, thick, woolly night-cap for yourselves and a balaclava for hubby. Don't forget to leave a hole for his mouth will you, or he will have the most dreadful problem disposing of his Horlicks. I think of everything don't I? You might think the idea of a night-cap a little silly, but let me tell you that an awful lot of hot air is lost through the top of the head. I know, because I lose an awful lot through the top of mine.

Now, if we work our way from top to bottom, how about wearing your pet cat round your neck at night to keep your neck warm? Dare I suggest a Siamese? It will match your hair won't it? Pullovers next, or sweaters as we call them in the Conservative Party. (Actually, Margaret calls them perspirers, but don't let on I told you for goodness' sake!)

As I said in my Reading address, I am a firm believer in long johns because they represent such good value for money. Not only can you wear them to keep warm, you can also cook suet puddings in them. How about this for a money-saving idea? Put your long johns on immediately after you have used them to cook puddings in, and get the benefit of the warmth; better still, wear them with the puddings still in them and get the best of both worlds!

Finally, we come to your little tootsies. As far as I'm concerned, there's no substitute for a good old hot water bottle. And if you can afford to put some hot water in it, then so much the better. I know one lady who put Horlicks in hers and when she woke up in the morning her foot had gone to sleep! (Not really, that's just my little joke. I exist only to make you happy).

Finally, can I pass on to you some advice my daddy used to give me when I was a little girl. Summer and winter, he was always shouting at me: "Wrap up, Edwina! For God's sake, wrap up!"

That's all for now my dears. See you next spring, I hope.

'WE MUST NOT BECOME SLAVES TO EUROCRATS'

[MAY 1988] - It is probably true to say that as far as most Britons are concerned, the Common Market is a distant irritation; an unwieldy foreign conspiracy that has proved itself economically unstable and administratively incompetent. It is an unsatisfactory mish-mash of half-baked compromises. If a camel is a horse designed by a committee, then a beef mountain is an agricultural policy designed by Eurocrats.

Therefore, it is manifestly not the sort of organisation of which Margaret Thatcher would wish to be an integral part, because it reminds her too much of the Britain she inherited in 1979.

Yet, when she points out these glaring deficiencies, and forthrightly declines an invitation for Britain to be lost in its bleak embrace, she is accused by her political adversaries for acting like 'a raving xenophobe' or 'rampaging across Europe like a soccer hooligan.' It would appear that some politicians are so unused to dealing in the truth, that they fail to recognise it when it comes in plain, unvarnished lumps.

Margaret Thatcher's attitude to the EEC being allowed to graduate from a commercial co-operative into a political union is sober and realistic. She knows full well that this high-falutin idealism will degenerate rapidly into a constitutional nightmare.

This incipient federalisation can be dismissed on two counts. Firstly, there is the motherland mentality to overcome. Britons - and I expect the same applies to Spaniards, Germans, Belgians etc - have a love for their own country that will never be transcended by an affection for the United States of Europe, no matter what material benefits may accrue.

Left-wing derision and displays of Right-wing vulgarity, in which drunken yobs swaddle themselves in the Union Jack, have combined to make patriotism a dirty word these days. Yet, in its purest form, it is a healthy emotion, and one so strong that thousands have laid down their lives in its name. Patriotism is the love of one's own country, not the unreasonable hatred of somebody else's. It is a multi-layered sense of belonging that is instinctive and manifests itself through events like the Olympics.

I am not ashamed to say that my greatest wish is to see an Isle of Wighter win a gold medal (yes, we have a contender in the table tennis). If he fails, then I would dearly love to see somebody from Portsmouth succeed. My priorities then progress to the south of England, England and then Britain. I could not care less how many the French or Germans win, and the creation of a supra-national institution embracing most of Europe will not make me feel any different in the future.

Patriotism also means an entirely logical affinity for familiar traditions and customs. It is a sense of feeling comfortable with your countrymen. That feeling is innate and cannot be denied. It is the reason, for example, why black people born and bred in this country support the West Indian cricket team when they tour.

The other - and more important - basis for Mrs Thatcher's hostility towards a federated Europe is the cumbersome bureaucracy it would inevitably create. Red tape, reinforced by national considerations, would be festooned around all of us. It would be the bunting of despair.

As the Prime Minister pointed out, there is a lesson to be learned from the Russian experience. Mikhail Gorbachev is desperately battling to dismantle the country's centralised and stagnant state control and disperse power to the regions. The irony of Europe attempting to trudge in the opposite direction was not lost on her.

It is almost certain that Margaret Thatcher's speech was a calculated response to the views of M Jacques Delors, President of the European Commission, who so enthralled the TUC in Bournemouth a fortnight ago with his talk of a continental paradise, where the European superstate would rule supreme and provide protection for the beleaguered trade unions.

While Mrs Thatcher is doing battle in Europe, however, she would do well to watch her back. All this talk of nationalism and separate identities is bound to attract the attention of the Welsh and Scottish nationalists, who are being denied that which she has now chosen to champion.

'DEPUTY LEADER NOBODY WANTS'

[OCTOBER 1987] - Roy Hattersley presents a pitiful sight at Labour Party conferences these days. He is the deputy leader for whom vast numbers are alleged to have voted, yet nobody seems to want. When the 'dream ticket' was resoundingly endorsed on the opening day of this year's gathering, Roy received 67 per cent of the available votes - almost three times as many as his nearest rival - yet he still looks like a hapless interloper in a foreign land.

When the result was announced, Neil Kinnock's exaggerated response was significant. He grinned broadly, pumped his colleague's hand and made an enormous fuss of mouthing the words: "I told you so." He produced every known congratulatory posture, short of ruffling Roy's hair, punching him playfully on the shoulder and leading a chorus of: "Here we go! Here we go! Here we go!"

This reaction indicates that Hattersley himself was not particularly confident of retaining the post, and his reception the morning after the night before proved his pessimism was well founded.

The conference was debating a document entitled *Democratic Socialist Aims and Values*, which had been written by Roy and amounted to his potted philosophy of the way forward for the Labour Party. It was rather like asking Ronald Reagan to rewrite the Koran, and its contents were taken personally by the 'Mikhail Gorbachev is a fascist' faction at the back of the hall.

They began by protesting that they could not hear what was being said, and ended by complaining bitterly because they could.

While the flak was flying from the body of the hall, Roy was busy with his impersonation of an infantryman on the Somme. Desperately worried, but trying to look brave, he occasionally stuck his head above the slit trench, remained there for a while with eyes flicking nervously from right to left, then quickly ducked back down when he sensed a sniper. Corporal Kinnock kept flashing an encouraging smile, which was met only by a wretched grimace. Still the shells exploded all around.

A delegate from Birmingham waved Roy's innermost thoughts in the air, declared them to be 'a load of waffle' and despaired of ever being able to explain them to her electorate.

Arthur Scargill, apparently recovered from the merciful silence that afflicted him during the TUC conference, bellowed his disapproval. He still clings to his quaint image of Britain that is populated only by destitute families on one hand and Porsche-driving stockbrokers on the other.

He mustered all the dirty words he could think of, like 'establishment collaborators' and 'mixed economy,' before snarling his contempt for a 'Yuppieland approach to run capitalism better than the Tories.' It was not, he said, what he had joined the Labour Party for. The most bitter denunciation came from a young man who regarded the document as 'a pompous, self-important, meaningless load of drivel.' It was the last comment before Roy rose to reply, and the words were still hanging in the air.

He did his best not to look pompous and self-important, but soon gave up when he realised the futility of trying to deny nature. Unerringly he told the comrades everything they did not wish to know; reminding them that socialism was not the doctrine of state control, and denouncing the worship of grand theory at the expense of pragmatism.

He harped on about the 'party of equality,' but one could sense the words falling silently around the heads of the freedom fighters from Liverpool and Brent East. They must have looked at Roy's £500 suit which barely encompassed his prosperous girth and smiled bleakly. Orwell, they no doubt thought, must have had Roy in mind when he spoke of some being more equal than others.

His speech ricocheted around an unresponsive auditorium and the rare bursts of applause sounded like jelly being dropped slowly into a galvanised bucket. He sat down to a smattering of indifference, and though the result of the eventual majority belied the hostility the motion had engendered, Roy and Neil must already be wondering just what the vote of confidence in their leadership actually means.

Could it be that when it really comes to the crunch, Roy and Neil will discover they have been given the freedom and the authority to do exactly what they are told?

'THE MERGER FROM WHICH ONLY CHAOS CAN NOW EMERGE'

[MAY 1987] - Forgive me for quoting myself, but I did say a couple of months back that the Liberals and Social Democrats seemed likely to merge into about five new parties. According to latest reports, I may have underestimated the number.

The fact is that any permanent union between the two was never going to be the cheerful accommodation of policies some thought. Had such a consensus ever existed, a separate SDP would never have been formed in 1981; its founders would simply have joined the Liberal Party. That they chose not to do so betrays a gulf in political thinking between the two groups that only David Owen and his followers considered unbridgeable and were prepared to acknowledge publicly.

Therefore, the best the new party (should it be formed) can hope to achieve is to formulate a charter built on mutually-acceptable policies, allow ideological differences to be seen but not heard and cement the whole shebang together by a joint determination to become the second force in British politics.

That is a rather hazardous premise on which to construct anything, let alone a political party, and the creaks are already beginning to be heard. It is not enough for senior members on both sides to treat them as nothing but bedding-in difficulties and blithely point out that both parties are 'a broad church' and should be big enough to accommodate thinking from both ends of the spectrum.

There is a fundamental flaw to this argument that cannot be ignored. Both the Conservative Party and the Labour Party have evolved into their present state over many years. Extremists in both regard the party as their own and are not prepared to abandon it to the other.

Does anyone honestly believe that if the Labour Party were to be launched from scratch tomorrow the views of Ken Livingstone and Bryan Gould could be realistically aligned under one banner? The thought is too preposterous to contemplate. And what about the Conservatives? Would Norman Tebbit and Ted Heath consider they had sufficient in common to help form a new political party? I doubt it.

Given these examples, why should it be any more likely for, say, Simon Hughes and Roy Jenkins to be compromised into an accord? Yet it is just this sort of unnatural compression of ideas and attitudes that activists of both the Liberal Party and the Social Democrats are being asked to accept. There is a chance that enough force will be exerted on both sides to cram everybody into the container, but how long the lid remains in place is another matter.

There can be no disputing the Liberal Party's mastery of petty politics - and this description is not intended to be as disparaging as it sounds. They are supreme manipulators of the local vote; enormously accomplished at attaining and retaining power at council level.

Thus, Liberal councillors form the party's power base. They are not merely big fish in a small pond, they are the only fish save for a few whale-sized MPs floating harmlessly around. Not only do they wield considerable influence, the majority are also extremists, as is the case with most activists in the other major parties. They have striven long and hard to shape the Liberal Party and though they would probably deny such a claim, many are content to beaver away at town hall level, convinced they will never accumulate enough votes to make any significant impact on the national scene anyway.

Liberals of my acquaintance (and believe it or not, I number at least two among my good friends) enjoy politics more than anybody else I know. Show me a Liberal let lose on a council election or better still, a by-election, and I will show you an animal in its natural habitat. However, show me a Liberal MP and I will show you a superficially jaunty but intrinsically insecure person, destined to wander forever in the strange nether world of position without power.

It is against this unique and daunting backcloth that the two parties are seeking to assemble a fit, streamlined, fighting unit ready to take on all-comers. At the moment they can't even agree upon a name. I wish them luck.

'NO FUTURE IN THE PAST FOR BENN AND HEFFER'

[MARCH 1988] - The first paragraph of *The Do-It-Yourself Manual for Political Fanatics*, states: "Unless you are convinced that everything you stand for is theoretically faultless and conceptually blameless, and unless you are prepared to eliminate all thoughts of personal culpability when involved in failure, do not bother to read any further."

I think we can safely say that Tony Benn skipped jauntily over those few words and ploughed on deep into the remainder of the book. Indeed, he may even have written it.

Mr Benn's Left-wing convictions, which have become more refined with each passing year, now manifest themselves in a variety of ways. There is the petulant debater, the thin-lipped martyr, the wide-eyed orator and the droning statistician. We are in for the entire repertoire this summer now he has decided to contest the Labour leadership.

Most of the characterisations were on display at the weekend, when he fired the first few random shots of the campaign. It was like watching an ancient Gatling gun creaking into action; plenty of noise but little impact. However, it was when asked precisely why he had chosen to enter a fight he was unlikely to win, that the real frailty of his case was exposed. "I am drawing attention," he said, "to the dangers of not being clear about what Mr Kinnock stands for. This is one of the reasons we lost in 1987 and it could be one of the major obstacles to victory in the next election."

No concession to personal responsibility you notice. Not the slightest indication that his own extremist rantings and those of his admirers might just have had a deterrent effect. Mr Benn believes that the purity of the Socialist dogma is at stake in the leadership struggle. He is convinced that if he can guide his party's policies back 40 years, disaffected Labour voters will flock to the banner.

He actually believes that at the last election millions of closet Socialists either threw in their lot with one of the other two main parties or else remained home in silent protest waiting for the messiah of Chesterfield to make his move.

Mr Benn is fond of telling us what 'the people' want. But who are these mythical millions? Indeed, where are these mythical millions? I will tell you. They are still roaming the minds of war-horses like Mr Benn and his running mate, Eric Heffer. They are sepia memories of stubborn old men, who will not believe that the days when thousands obeyed the factory hooter to down tools, unscrew a flask of tea and read the *Daily Herald* are long gone.

The Labour Party's poll fodder of days gone by has dissipated, to be replaced by a mixture of zealots, diehards and trendies. The problem with Tony Benn and his ilk is that they listen to the committed individual bellowing directly into their ear and ignore the far-off murmurings of the majority. On the rare occasions that the seed of doubt is sown, they sustain each other with thin war cries and empty promises.

Mr Benn asks us to believe that the policies now belatedly commending themselves to Neil Kinnock - like multi-lateral disarmament, realistic trades union legislation and denationalisation - are a betrayal of Socialist principles and have no support in the country. He is wrong on both counts. What he really means is that such policies are a betrayal of Tony Benn's principles and he therefore blindly believes them to have no support in the country.

He conveniently forgets (or ignores) the fact that the Labour Party is the political wing of the trades union movement and that in recent elections union members have voted overwhelmingly against archaic Socialist tenets. The party must therefore move to accommodate this new mood, not stick intractably to some antediluvian creed.

Neil Kinnock realises that his party must now make hasty moves to rejoin the electorate which began to abandon it ideologically in the mid-seventies. He knows those millions will not be persuaded to turn back or even stop, so the race is on to catch them up. It is a difficult journey for Kinnock and the only favour Tony Benn has done him is to choose to fight now and not in two years' time. It enables the Labour leader to squash the Hard Left and still have enough time left to mount a serious challenge for Downing Street.

'A MASTER OF COMPROMISE'

[JULY 1988] - Paddy Ashdown has made his name as an extreme moderate; a man who cannot hear an argument without rushing in with a compromise solution. In the process he has become the political equivalent of Polyfilla.

In fairness to the man, it is impossible for anyone to survive in, let alone become master of, a party like the SLD without first mastering the art of conciliation. As soon as you express a firm opinion on anything, there is a danger of being branded Conservative or Socialist because the fence on which social democrats perch is a fragile structure.

Typical of the SLD (or Salads as they are becoming known) is the name they have chosen for themselves. They were a new party and could have chosen a new name. Predictably, the urge for rapprochement got the better of them all and they came up with an uninspiring concoction which possessed the twin characteristics of being both forgettable and guaranteed to confuse.

Paddy Ashdown is believed to have favoured the name 'The Democrats' but he did not push too hard at the time because a man striving to be leader could not run the risk of alienating both factions within the party before the contest had even begun. There is a chance of course that now Ashdown has his hands firmly on the rein he will consider it his duty to steer all the horses in the same direction. It is already becoming clear, however, that he will need more than a tug on the bit to control a few of them.

He has already stated that one of his party's objectives must be to overtake Labour. This has already met with some opposition from members who insist the prime intention should be to overtake the Conservatives. One would have thought that if the SLD managed to overhaul the Conservatives they would automatically have bypassed Labour, but apparently it is not quite as simple as that.

This argument, which is brewing just in time for the party's first conference next month, concerns the direction the Social and Liberal Democrats should take. Should they target themselves at disaffected Socialists or conscience-stricken Conservatives? Who they happen to overtake en route (if anyone at all) is purely incidental.

The essential struggle within the SLD, therefore, revolves around the question of whether it should be centre Right (a philosophy espoused by the likes of Alan Beith) or centre Left (which appeals to Ashdown and his supporters.

It does not appear to have occurred to them that the only chance they have of becoming a respected force in national politics is to formulate policies which pay no obeisance to either side of the political spectrum. Pursuing temporary solutions in order to woo the supporters of one particular rival party is both cheap and ultimately futile.

It stands to reason that whatever course they plot will be influenced to a certain degree by policies already adopted by the two main parties, because there are few completely new ideas left in politics. It is impossible to be a centre party and not suffer this inconvenience, but there is a world of difference between that and deliberately doctoring ideas in order to attract a specific section of society.

The trouble with the SLD supporters is that they are desperately anxious not to offend. They cannot bear the thought that anyone may find them unlovely. They are still loath to accept that politics is an ugly business and believe that common sense and concord will always prevail in the end. They don't (and as a millennium full of wars will confirm) they probably never will.

When the SLD stops believing it can be all things to everyone and realises it will have to make real enemies in order to make true friends, people will begin to take it seriously as a political force.

Until that time they will always be fondly regarded but ultimately ignored.

CHAPTER TWELVE

The man who left Robert Maxwell fuming

AS I COMPLETE this book I am coming to the end of my 37th year in provincial journalism. It has been a period of momentous change. Just how convulsive was brought home to me by a friend who pointed out that if William Caxton had come to life in the late seventies he would still have had a reasonable grasp of the printing process. Had he returned a few years later he would have considered himself to be stranded in a world of sorcery, where nothing made sense anymore and newspapers were produced as if by magic by information that travelled not by paper and hot lead across a single building, but by invisible signals across an entire country and beyond.

There are many people working in the industry today who would identify with Caxton's bemusement. Computers have certainly introduced an element of wizardry into the production of newspapers, but when all the fancy tricks go wrong the frustration is immense.

When I started back in the mid-sixties some printers underwent a seven-year apprenticeship and the vast majority of them were as literate and well-read as any journalist. Indeed, there was nothing they enjoyed more than pointing out our mistakes, and those who became 'readers' (checkers of copy) were scrupulously professional and took any mistake they failed to spot as a personal insult.

Compositors were proud craftsmen who often wore a shirt and tie. As a youngster I often wondered how they managed to do up the buttons because the ends of their fingers had been rendered calloused and insensitive by years of pressing home slugs of type and leading as they hovered over the pages into which they poured the utmost effort, care and professionalism.

Now their job is no more. It was swept aside years ago by technological advancement that should not always be confused with progress. A reporter's story once passed through up to three different pairs of knowledgeable hands before it reached the page. It was subbed, set and proof-read. Now it goes straight from the terminal to a sub-editor and on to the page. The long-stops have long gone and with them the opportunity to pick up the kind of mistakes that will always be made, whether through carelessness or ignorance.

The papers of the sixties and seventies were far more labour-intensive and it was an industry ripe for cost-cutting on the back of new technology.

That duly arrived and companies became far more profitable. But at what price? Newspapers - including those in the regions - undoubtedly look better than they have ever done. But who buys a newspaper for the attractiveness of its design?

When was the last time you heard of anyone going into a newsagents and saying: "I'll have a newspaper my good woman. The finest-looking one in the shop if you please." People buy certain newspapers because they are comfortable with them, they trust them, they empathise with their general editorial thrust. They are familiar companions. They know where everything is going to be and what the structure of the newspaper will be like from one week to the next.

So why do so many new editors mark their arrival on a title by ordering a complete redesign? They are like skunks marking their territory, ensuring that everyone will know where they have been irrespective of the unpleasantness it leaves behind them. It is a vain and preposterous thing to do. Newspapers should be tweaked and massaged; they should be allowed to evolve gently so that everyone connected with them, from writers to readers, is at ease with what is happening.

Classic evidence of this is provided by the *Daily Mail*. From a sales point of view it has been the fastest-growing newspaper of recent years because successive editors David English and Paul Dacre invested in quality writers rather than design boffins. The *Mail* looks quite different now to what it did in the mid-eighties, but no-one has noticed the change. It has been subtle, unobtrusive and secondary to the content. By adopting this approach it has carried along its established core of readers and attracted new ones. It is an object lesson for those who believe in change for the sake of it.

There have been some improvements that have been welcomed by the industry at every level. Foremost among them is the widespread availability of full colour, yet I remember some respected editors (especially those in charge of long-established provincial titles) resisting its introduction for sound yet short-sighted reasons. They believed that it would prove too garish and cheapen their newspaper, and for a while they looked like being proved right.

I remember chatting to former *Daily Mirror* editor Derek Jameson, and he recalled when he was in charge of the title's Irish edition when full-colour presses first came on line.

"I couldn't bloody well believe it," he bellowed. (He wasn't angry. He always bellowed). "Photographers, most of whom I had previously regarded as perfectly sane people, started sending me endless pictures of clowns standing in the middle of fields of daffodils beneath a bright blue sky. They were like kids who had been given a brand-new box of crayons and couldn't resist scribbling everywhere. It took a fair old time before they realised you took a picture because the content was right, not because it had a lot of different colours in it."

The proliferation of alternative sources of information has had a detrimental effect on the sales of provincial daily newspapers, and it is hardly surprising. They are no longer the sole providers of local news and information every 24 hours. They now have to contend with local radio and television stations, teletext and the internet. News is available on demand and in forms that are far more convenient.

As a kid working as a district reporter for *The News* at Portsmouth, I remember seeing some people buy up to four copies of the same newspaper in one afternoon. Why? Because it was the only way they could find out the racing results. It seems ridiculous now, but back in the sixties the results would be phoned through to the office manager, he would transfer them to the bush machine (on which the stop press was printed) run some copies through and immediately sell them to men waiting in the shop. Half an hour later they would be back again. This sort of thing had a healthy if misleading influence on sales, but it helps people understand why the fifties and sixties were the heyday of provincial evenings in particular.

It was the same with their Saturday evening football specials. We are now bombarded with information from so many different sources that it seems impossible to believe that up until the eighties there were few places to obtain a full list of football results. If you missed Sports Report on the radio at 5pm on Saturday evenings, or the teleprinter on *Grandstand*, your next hope was the local sports paper. It was quite common for people to queue outside the newsagents and await the arrival of the sports edition. As a kid on the Isle of Wight, I can certainly recall many a winter's evening spent in the queue waiting for the old *Football Mail* to arrive. If the *Sports Echo* based in Southampton turned up first it was ignored. Pompey fans like us would never dream of reading it, no matter how desperate we were to check out the classified results.

Now the details are but a bleep and a click away any time of the day and night, but it is a testimony to people's natural affection for local newspapers that despite this immediate and widespread availability of electronic information, the sales of many Saturday night sports editions - especially in areas like Portsmouth where support for the local football club borders on the fanatical - remain buoyant.

This is a bonus to those of us coming to the end of our newspaper careers and who find the very concept of websites anathema and the remorseless evolution of new technology baffling and often deeply irritating.

It is always there to trap the unwary, as my colleague Peter Homer discovered. Peter is probably the most accomplished and professional journalist I have ever known at a local level and he immediately saw the benefits of the internet when it came to shoring up stories with background information. For example, when he discovered that a neglected house in Chichester had once been the home of author Anna Sewell he immediately launched a search to find out more about her. Unfortunately, the words he provided for the search engine were 'Black Beauty' and Ms Sewell did not get a mention until entry number 348. It was, as a flustered Peter later confirmed, educational.

The main objection I have to newspaper websites is that they give you everything for free. That goes against the grain to someone who has spent all their life placing a value on what they do. The received wisdom is that websites play their part in enhancing the interest in the printed products, but I have my doubts.

I always point to *The Guardian* to back up my argument. By common consensus it has by the far the finest website of any national newspaper. You can access it for free and read everything that appears in the printed version - only sooner. However, sales of the printed version itself continue to struggle. As the Americans might say - go do the math.

About ten years ago a former colleague visited Japan and came back burbling with enthusiasm for what he had found. Within 15 years or even less, he assured us, newspapers as we know them now will begin to disappear. Instead, people will purchase little screens that they will take with them wherever they go and on which they would be able to download any newspaper to which they had subscribed.

Not only that, the pictures wouldn't just be stills they would be moving and readers would be able to stop the action, rewind it and play it as often as they liked. Think of the benefits that would bring to sports coverage he said. Everything would be updated at the touch of a button. We nodded knowingly at each other behind his back, smiled sympathetically and pointed our index fingers at our temple while making that little circular motion that denotes dottiness in others.

But he was right. This era is upon us. The technology is now in place and some of the newest mobile phones are beginning to provide the rudiments of something that even a short time ago was considered too fantastical to be true.

My generation will continue to pay lip-service to this 'progress.' We will invest in some of the gadgetry and then sit by helpless while our children or grandchildren show us which buttons to press. But it doesn't mean we have to look forward to the day or rejoice when it arrives. For me it will be a sad though strangely privileged moment. It will mean that my career will have spanned an era in what we now refer to as the 'communications industry' in which the changes that have taken place can only be described as unsurpassed.

But as with all transforming periods of this magnitude, there has been a cost as well as a benefit. Jobs have disappeared, entire professions have been erased and with them have gone some of the characters and idiosyncrasies that made newspapers such a special environment in which to work.

A natural instinct when writing a book of this kind is to mull over the past and come up with the special memories. For example, my favourite career moment was not being fortunate enough to receive a few awards. No, it was the day I covered a Portsmouth Football Club match for the one and only time.

Because of illness and holidays, I was the only one left on the sports desk at the end of the week deemed capable of covering a Pompey match at Fratton Park. All the others were sub-editors, so I was dispatched to report on a team I had supported since my father took me to the ground for the first time 20 years earlier to watch Billy Wright and his all-conquering Wolves' side of the fifties. My father was not a man given to displays of emotion - his generation tended not to be - but when I phoned him that morning to let him know what was happening I could almost hear his chest puff out at the other end of the line.

Doing a running story (phoning your words to a copy typist while the match is going on) is a fraught business. Then you face the prospect of doing a considered piece for the following Monday's newspaper. It's a wonderful job for any sports-loving reporter, but it's certainly not an easy one. It doesn't help either if you find yourself cheering on your team in the professional sanctity of the press box. Least impressed was the typist at the other end of the line who said the noise went through her like a hot needle.

However, I managed to mug my way through and on leaving the Press box I saw, at the bottom of the stairs looking up at me, my old chap with some of his mates from the Isle of Wight. I'll never forget the proud expression on his face and it was obvious that had I gone on to win the Nobel Prize for Literature it would have meant nothing to him compared with that moment.

I have always had a fondness for anecdotes. I tend to remember them long after more important information has been scoured from my brain. The newspaper industry is full of them, and my favourite was told to me by a former colleague Chris Bisco, who had spent a hairy few months working as one of Robert Maxwell's financial team. Chris swears it is true.

Apparently Maxwell was fervently opposed to his employees smoking and when striding through his headquarters with the usual team in tow one morning he happened upon a man lounging against a corridor wall puffing on a cigarette. He was incandescent.

"You," boomed the old fraudster. "How much do you earn in a month?"

"About two grand Mr Maxwell," replied the man.

Maxwell stopped and ordered one of his team to open up a briefcase he was carrying and he carefully counted out £4,000 in £100 pound notes.

"Here, take this," he bellowed at the errant smoker. "Now get out of my sight and never let me see you in this building again."

"Thanks very much," said the man, and scampered out of the building as quickly as he could. He was a Post Office engineer and had only popped in to deliver a new handset.

I wouldn't have done any other job. Indeed, I cannot conceive of any other job that I would have wanted to do (except a professional cricketer, and you had to have talent for that) or been qualified to undertake.

But now that the finishing line is in sight, I can't say I'm sorry. It's been a lot of fun and I've had plenty of laughs on the basis that if you are lucky you spend most of your life at work and if you don't have a laugh it means you spend a lot of your life miserable.

That is why I offer up thanks for people like the Chichester man who used to pop into the *Observer* office at regular intervals to explain how he had managed to set Pythagoras theorems to music.

But that's another story...

PHOTOGRAPHS

It's a pity the camera never lies

MY FAMILY SUGGESTED this chapter should be called 'Newbery - The Hair Years' for the fairly obvious reason that when most of these photographs were taken I actually had some. I convince myself that I have become glabrous in the cause of journalism, and if stress is indeed a contributory factor to natural depilation there may be more truth in this forlorn hope than I imagine.

To begin with, I had my photograph taken with people like Jimmy Savile because I wanted to prove to my mates that I had actually met him. Then I wanted to be photographed with people like Britt Ekland because she was, in every way, a gorgeous person. Then I had to have my photograph taken because I was fortunate enough to receive some awards that were presented by well-known people.

But after a while it becomes tedious because journalists - even those from the sticks where the stardust tends to linger slightly longer in the eyes - tend to get a little blase about appearing in their own newspapers. Friends and relatives become positively insolent. "See you were in the paper again last week. Don't be tempted to rob a bank. You're starting to look just like one of those photofit pictures..."

The photographs in this chapter had to be unearthed from beneath years of accumulated attic debris. I am just not the type to keep albums and even if I did I would rarely look at them because there is nothing more depressing and pointless than monitoring the passing of the years.

These days I couldn't care less whether my photograph is taken or not. Mind you, if I ever got the chance to interview Jamie Lee-Curtis or Alison Hanney (CJ in the wonderful *West Wing*) I might be prepared to give the matter further consideration...

The Princess Royal did the honours at the Regional Press Awards in 1988, and though I've never been in her company before or since she seemed remarkably at ease considering the odium in which she is said to hold journalists. We had a bit of a laugh when she asked me what sports I wrote about, and I told her anything that didn't involve horses. She said she would arrange for me to be more comfortable around the beasts, but I'm still waiting for the invitation to Gatcombe Park.

It's a tough job interviewing the famous, but people like Britt Ekland sometimes made it worthwhile. The photographer on this trip sat in silent admiration for the first 15 minutes and when he eventually spoke it made her jump. I think she thought I was a ventriloquist.

This picture was taken at Newport Conservative Club in the run-up to the 1979 election. Note the Thatcher stare.
She never took her eyes off mine for the entire conversation, and her idea of small talk was to ask questions like: "And what do you think are among the foremost deleterious effects of the Common Agricultural Policy?"
The Conservative candidate at the time, Dudley Fishburn, appears to be wearing an expression which says: "Go on then cleverdick - answer the lady."

This was the first time I met one of my heroes, Hugh Cudlipp. Our paths were to cross again years later when he chaired a discussion on newspapers in Chichester Cathedral and I was a member of the panel.

These pictures on the *Coronation Street* set are among my most treasured possessions.

There's top producer John Temple showing me the sights, and me posing like mad outside the Rovers Return and what was then Alf Roberts' corner shop.

The late Bill Waddington, a charming man, couldn't help but adopt his Percy Sugden alter ego, and that rather modest little area with the sign 'Julie's Place' hanging on the wall was the personal domain of Miss Goodyear who played Bet Lynch.

ALFRED ROBERTS

NEWTON
&
RIDLEY
ROVERS RETURN INN

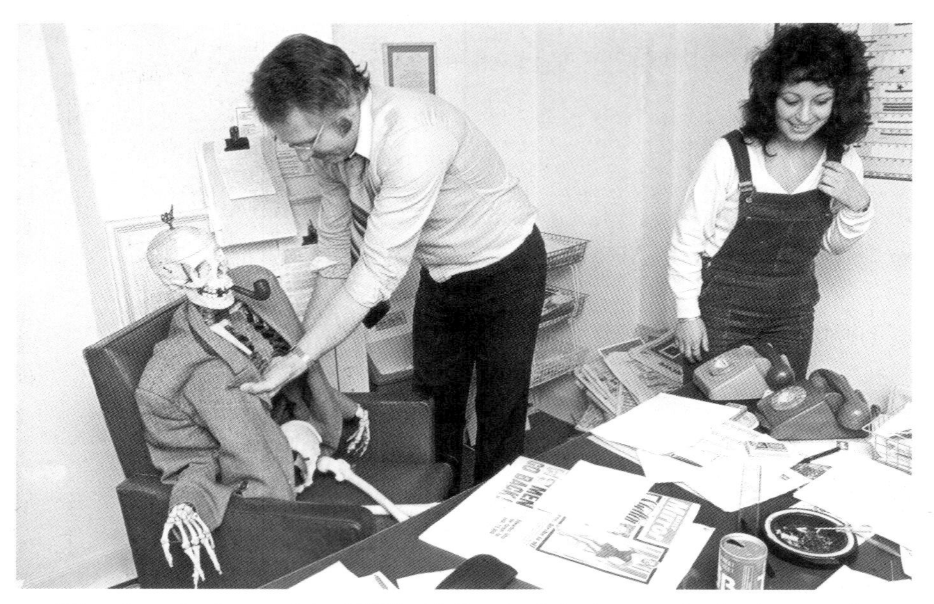

When I was in charge of the *IW Weekly Post* back in the seventies, having a laugh was often part of the working day. On one occasion I borrowed a life-size skeleton from the local hospital, which Murray Sanders and I managed to smuggle into the building. Junior reporter Zoe McIntyre (pictured) worked in the office downstairs, so Murray and I sat the skeleton in my chair, dressed it in my jacket and tie and taped my pipe to its mouth.

I then rang down to Zoe from the office next door and told her I wasn't feeling too well. She immediately offered to get me some pills but I told her it was probably nothing and that it would pass. Three minutes later I rang again and said in gasping tones: "Zoe, I'm feeling like death. You'd better come up quickly!"

She raced up the stairs and burst into my office. The ensuing scream alerted most of lower Ryde and when Murray and I appeared from next door convulsed with laughter, poor Zoe was trembling uncontrollably. That may look like a smile in the photograph, but take it from me - it was the remains of a terrified grin.

I received this British Sports Journalism Award in 1994 from Trevor Brooking, who was a member of the judging panel. I remember thinking that my entry the previous year had been better, but then remembered it included an article critical of Mr Brooking. Great player in his day, but not one of the country's most naturally gifted communicators.

I won't be the first (nor the last I suspect) to observe that Jimmy Savile is a strange man. When we met at a holiday camp on the Isle of Wight he was friendly in a distant and careful sort of way, chatted for a long time and said absolutely nothing. What you see is certainly not what you get with Mr Savile.

If Radio 4's resident psychiatrist Dr Anthony Clare admitted he was unable to penetrate the shield Savile has carefully constructed around himself, what hope did I have?

Critic of the Year

Clive James, *The Observer*

Commended
Nancy Banks-Smith, *The Guardian*
Herbert Kretzmer, *Daily Mail*
Keith Newbery, *The News, Portsmouth*

My hero! The year was 1981 and there I was in the running for the British Press Awards Critic of the Year competition which was won, of course, by Clive James. But just to see my name in the same programme as him, Nancy Banks-Smith and Herbert Kretzmer was reward enough.

This is another photograph that I hope never to lose. It was a particular pleasure to receive this Regional Press Award from John Humphrys because he remains the doyen of all interviewers. He is head and shoulders above his contemporaries because it is impossible to detect where his political sympathies lie. I shudder to think where the exercise of open democracy would be without him.

We brought the traffic to a standstill outside the *Weekly Post* office in Union Street, Ryde, when Rod Hull brought Emu along. He had been hired to open the *Weekly Post* motor show at a time when he was at the height of his popular appeal. Rod Hull himself was a quiet, almost unprepossessing man who was extremely agreeable, especially to children, even when the cameras were not trained on him.

I remember talking to him in my office before he went out to greet the huge crowd that had gathered, and he seemed genuinely perplexed and humbled by his appeal. But as soon as he got to grips with the emu puppet it was almost as if he had something behind which to hide his awkwardness. They melded into one entertainment package and as he made his way through our office to the street. It was fascinating to watch the way in which everyone instinctively backed away.

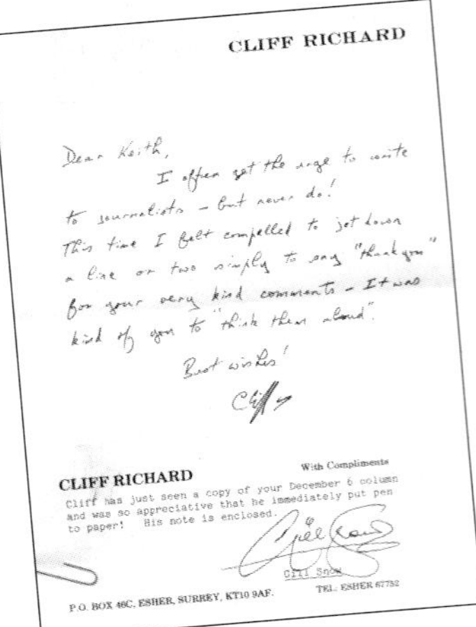

CLIFF RICHARD

Dear Keith,
I often get the urge to write to journalists – but never do!
This time I felt compelled to jot down a line or two simply to say "thank you" for your very kind comments – It was kind of you to "think them aloud".
Best wishes!
Cliff

CLIFF RICHARD
With Compliments
Cliff has just seen a copy of your December 6 column and was so appreciative that he immediately put pen to paper! His note is enclosed.
Gill Snow
P.O. BOX 46C, ESHER, SURREY, KT10 9AF. TEL: ESHER 67752

This letter arrived out of the blue from Cliff Richard. Apparently he had got to see a copy of a column I had written about him, in which I pointed out that though his music was not to my taste I appreciated a talent that had obviously been honed and perfected over the years. I was a nice of him to write but I remember thinking at the time that it was strange that someone so famous could be so grateful to a small-town hack who had taken the trouble to say something pleasant about him.

To my left are Murray Sanders and Richard Wright, the photographer and reporter who once took it upon themselves to rescue a 'lost' sheepdog on the hottest day of the year (see chapter 6). They are another two who don't look a day older than when this picture was taken in 1984. People reckon it must be something to do with the Isle of Wight air, but how come it never worked for me? The chap on the left is Chris Thwaites, now chief photographer on the *IW County Press*.

When I joined *The News Portsmouth* in 1984 as associate editor with responsibility for sport and features I inherited this great crowd of people. In the checked shirt at the back, smiling as usual, is Alister Marshall, a man given to writing premature obituaries. Next to him is Reg Betts, a man not unacquainted with suffering and next to him is Pete Smith, my cohort in an April Fool's joke we played on the local constabulary.

Next to me in the back row is Mike Neasom, a workaholic who once covered a Pompey match in Carlisle, drove back through the night, went straight into the office and had the story already written for the first edition. Next to him is Nigel Peake, a talented man who had the sense to get out of journalism and earn some real money. From the left in the front row are Les Rothery, Chris Stratford, Annie England, Beryl Jobling, Phil Tusler and the inimitable Alan Montgomery, once rumoured to have finished runner-up in a competition run by The Bobby Darin Quiff Appreciation Society.

This is the relatively small band of people who were doing their best to disturb the dominance of the *County Press* on the Isle of Wight when we launched the *Weekly Post* in the seventies. They were a great bunch, but sadly some are no longer with us. Michael (Bruce) Eldridge, seen on the extreme left of the photograph, who was our driver-mechanic, had been a friend of mine since childhood and he died only this year.

On my immediate right, pipe to the fore as usual, is deputy editor Keith Huyton who also died quite recently. This tough old Yorkshireman was an invaluable ally and on one press day sat there subbing pages after having just had a tooth removed. He held a huge handkerchief to his mouth with one hand to staunch the flow of blood while did his work with the other.

He only agreed to go home when the hankie became so sodden with blood that it was running down his sleeve. Without the help of people like that we would never have got the paper out sometimes. I always remember having a discussion with Keith once about nuclear war, and as usual he had a firm opinion on the subject. "Nay lad," he said, "a bloody nuclear war doesn't hold any fears for me for the simple reason that I don't intend to survive one."

On my immediate left is advertising manager Paul Dyer, who is still a good friend and, worryingly, doesn't look a day older now than when this photograph was taken.

They were a great bunch and 25 years down the line this is my thank you to them.

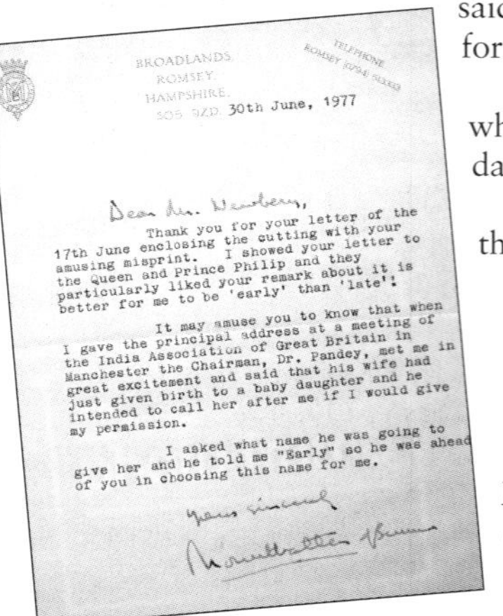

BROADLANDS,
ROMSEY,
HAMPSHIRE.
SO5 9ZD. 30th June, 1977

TELEPHONE
ROMSEY (0794) 5XXXX

Dear Mr. Newbery,

Thank you for your letter of the 17th June enclosing the cutting with your amusing misprint. I showed your letter to the Queen and Prince Philip and they particularly liked your remark about it is better for me to be 'early' than 'late'!

It may amuse you to know that when I gave the principal address at a meeting of the India Association of Great Britain in Manchester the Chairman, Dr. Pandey, met me in great excitement and said that his wife had just given birth to a baby daughter and he intended to call her after me if I would give my permission.

I asked what name he was going to give her and he told me "Early" so he was ahead of you in choosing this name for me.

Yours sincerely

Mountbatten of Burma

This is the letter written to me by Lord Mountbatten and it rates as the ultimate in name-dropping. "I showed your letter to the Queen and Prince Philip..." indeed.

These are some of the awards I have managed to accrue over the years. Funny thing about newspaper awards - they spend a fortune on food and drink and a couple of bob on framed certificates or lumps of perspex. Still, it's the thought that counts.

You can't beat the humour and buzz of a newsroom, whether it be on *Drop the Dead Donkey* or at the hub of a county weekly like the *Chichester Observer*. The laughs are usually at someone else's expense and the work can be hard and hectic, but once you've sampled the atmosphere there's nothing quite like it.

Incidentally, the chap hard at work to my immediate right while I have a ponder is Peter Homer - the finest general reporter I've ever had the privilege of working with.

Index